Faith
OF OUR FATHERS
A STUDY OF HEBREWS 11

Marshall McDaniel

Copyright © 2025 One Stone Press. All rights reserved. No part of this book may be reproduced in any form without written permission of the publisher.

Unless otherwise marked, scripture quotations are taken from the NEW AMERICAN STANDARD BIBLE® (NASB), Copyright © 1960, 1962, 1963, 1968, 1971, 1972, 1973, 1975, 1977, 1995 by The Lockman Foundation. Used by permission. www.Lockman.org.

Scripture quotations marked DRB are taken from the Douay-Rheims Bible (1899), public domain.

Scripture quotations marked ESV are taken from The ESV® Bible (The Holy Bible, English Standard Version®), Copyright © 2001 by Crossway, a publishing ministry of Good News Publishers. Used by permission. All rights reserved.

Scripture quotations marked NET are taken from NET Bible®, Copyright © 1996–2016 by Biblical Studies Press, L.L.C. http://netbible.com. Used by permission. All rights reserved.

Scripture quotations marked NIV are taken from the Holy Bible, New International Version®, NIV®. Copyright © 1973, 1978, 1984, 2011 by Biblica, Inc.TM Used by permission of Zondervan. All rights reserved worldwide. www.zondervan.com. The "NIV" and "New International Version" are trademarks registered in the United States Patent and Trademark Office by Biblica, Inc.TM

Scripture quotations marked NKJV are taken from the New King James Version®. Copyright © 1982 by Thomas Nelson. Used by permission. All rights reserved.

Scripture quotations marked NLT are taken from the Holy Bible, New Living Translation, Copyright © 1996, 2004, 2015 by Tyndale House Foundation. Used by permission of Tyndale House Publishers, Inc., Carol Stream, Illinois 60188. All rights reserved.

Scripture quotations marked NRSV are taken from the New Revised Standard Version Bible, Copyright © 1989 National Council of the Churches of Christ in the United States of America. Used by permission. All rights reserved worldwide.

Design by Stephen Sebree / Moonlight Graphic Works

Published by One Stone Press
979 Lovers Lane
Bowling Green, KY 42103

Printed in the United States of America

ISBN-13: 978-1-966992-00-4

Dedication 5

Introduction 7

Lesson 1: **Faith Starts and Ends with God** — Introduction 9

Lesson 2: **Faith Offers Everything to God** — Abel 15

Lesson 3: **Faith Walks with God** — Enoch 21

Lesson 4: **Faith Fears God** — Noah 27

Lesson 5: **Faith Trusts the Promises of God** — Abraham (Part 1) 33

Lesson 6: **Faith Trusts the Promises of God** — Abraham (Part 2) 39

Lesson 7: **Faith Submits to God** — Isaac and Jacob 45

Lesson 8: **Faith Hopes in God** — Joseph 51

Lesson 9: **Faith Stands with God** — Moses 57

Lesson 10: **Faith Waits on God** — Moses, Joshua, and Israel 63

Lesson 11: **Faith Gives New Life in God** — Rahab 69

Lesson 12: **Faith Prevails and Perseveres for God** — Judges, Kings,
 Prophets, and Saints 75

Lesson 13: **Faith Focuses on God** — Jesus 81

Conclusion 87

Works Consulted 89

DEDICATION

To Grey Sebree. I never got the chance to know you, but your reputation of faithfulness echoes to the present. Like the "heroes" of Hebrews 11, you still speak (Hebrews 11:4). Though we did not meet in this life, I count it a privilege to call your parents, Steve and Debbie, my friends. Their dedication to the Lord and to his people makes them Hebrews-11 heroes in my book. I do not know how long it will be before I catch up with you and finish the race, but I look forward to seeing you at the finish line (12:1–2).

The author-proceeds from the sale of this workbook are being donated to the Grey Sebree Sacred Selections memoriam. To learn more about Grey and the fund that honors his life, visit www.sacredselections.org/grey-sebree.

INTRODUCTION

"I love passages like this!" Greg said during a Sunday afternoon Bible study, "These kinds of stories really help me appreciate the humanity and faith of the people in the Bible." I love Greg's sentiment. The people of the Old and New Testaments were actual people. They faced the same sorts of challenges that we face, and they exercised real faith, faith that we need to emulate. They were not perfect, but they were faith-filled people who relied on the Lord. Hebrews 11 catalogues several faithful individuals, the best and the worst of them, confirming the statement of David Young: "God uses imperfect people who are in imperfect situations to do his perfect will." Scripture is full of these kinds of stories, and God expects us to learn from them. The Bible says, "For whatever was written in earlier times was written for our instruction, so that through perseverance and the encouragement of the Scriptures we might have hope" (Romans 15:4). When we read the stories of faithful people—like Abraham, Moses, and David—and serve the Lord as they did, their hope will be ours. Just as God helped them through the good and the bad, so he will do for us.

The stories of Old Testament believers (and unbelievers) are examples for us (1 Corinthians 10:6, 11). The Greek word translated "example" (*typos*) in 1 Corinthians 10 indicates that we should pattern our lives after the good and avoid the bad. Their successes and failures show us what pleases and displeases God. The writer of Hebrews understood the value of Old Testament examples. At the end of Hebrews 10, he highlighted the future-looking, perseverant nature of faith (Hebrews 10:35–39; see Lesson 1). He then illustrated this faith in real people—Abel, Enoch, Noah, Abraham, just to name the first of many. Some interpreters label this section of Scripture "The Roll Call of the Faithful" or "The Hall of Faith." The author of Hebrews does not set these people up as "super believers who possessed faith reserved for a select few" but as men and women who exercised authentic faith in God-honoring ways.

In this study, we will traverse the faith-landscape of Hebrews 11, learning from these individuals who put their trust in God. We will see that faith does not equal sinless perfection; rather, faith is how we connect with the only one who is perfect, God. In each lesson, we will highlight a particular aspect of faith in each of the following Bible characters: Abel will teach us about righteousness, Enoch about devotion, and Noah about reverence; we will see the conviction of Abraham, the perspective of Isaac and Jacob, and the hope of Joseph; Moses will impress us with his loyalty to God, and he (Moses), Joshua, and Israel will show us what perseverance really looks like; Rahab, the judges, the kings, and the prophets—as well as several other unnamed "heroes"—will help us see that faith works and that it fights for what is right. And last, but certainly not least, we will meet the author and finisher of faith, Jesus Christ himself, celebrate his victory, and fix our eyes on him forever.

We need these examples of faith. Why? Because we need all the help we can get as we grow in faithfulness to God. Anything less than real faith disappoints and destroys us. Yet, when we genuinely believe, we can confidently face life on this side of eternity. Do you and I long for this kind of faith? If so, then we need to spend some time with our "fathers" and "mothers" in the faith, the believers of Hebrews 11.

Marshall McDaniel, 2025

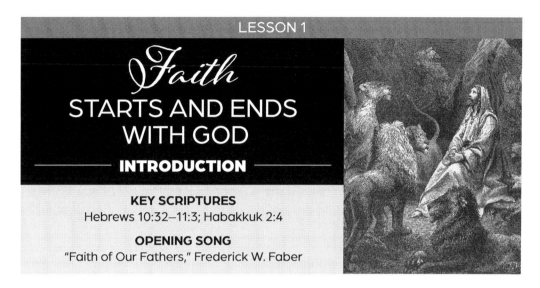

LESSON 1

Faith Starts and Ends with God

INTRODUCTION

KEY SCRIPTURES
Hebrews 10:32–11:3; Habakkuk 2:4

OPENING SONG
"Faith of Our Fathers," Frederick W. Faber

Imagine you are a Jewish Christian living during the reign of Nero (c. AD 54–68). You have heard that the sadistic Roman ruler is targeting anyone who worships Jesus. The report does not surprise you, for Nero's slate is far from clean. You know persecution is coming, so you must make a choice: side with Caesar and live, or hold tight to Jesus and suffer and perhaps even die! Early on in your faith, you sacrificed anything and everything for the cause of Christ. But times have changed. Your faith has changed. The choice is not as easy as it once was. What will you do? Will your loyalty to God pass this test? These questions fill your mind. But then a letter from a trusted source arrives, labeled simply "To the Hebrews," and it exhorts you to persevere.

Obviously, parts of the preceding paragraph are somewhat speculative but perhaps not too far off the historical mark. The recipients were in (or were fast approaching) a time of trial, and their faith was on the line. Over and over, the author of Hebrews admonishes his readers to persevere, not just to maintain the status quo but to move forward in a mature, God-honoring way (e.g., Hebrews 2:1–4; 5:11–6:3; 10:19–25, 35–39; 12:1–3). Why does he do so? Because he knows that faithfulness pleases God and that faithlessness does not.

How can we know if our faith honors God and meets his approval? The examples in Hebrews 11 provide a metric for self-evaluation. But before we can learn from these faithful men and women, we must first consider the context and the definition of biblical faith. In this lesson, we will examine the last section of Hebrews 10 and the first part of Hebrews 11 to determine the kind of faith that God rewards, namely a perseverant, confident, and active loyalty to him. We, like the "heroes" of Hebrews 11, can be faithful, but we must start and end with God; for he is the author and perfecter of faith (12:1–2).

THE GREAT REWARD OF FAITH

The author of Hebrews begins with the end in mind, with the consequence of God-pleasing faith—the "great reward" (Hebrews 10:35). The recipients of Hebrews had, early in their walk with Christ, readily sacrificed their possessions (6:10; 10:32–34; see 13:3). The writer reminds them that their eternal prize far outstrips their present pain (10:35; see Romans 8:18). The Greek word translated "reward" (*misthapodosia*) in Hebrews 10:35 occurs three times in the New Testament (Hebrews 2:2; 10:35; 11:26) and means compensation, recompense, or wages paid in return for work done (BDAG, s.v. "μισθαποδοσία"). The author is not denying the grace of God; he is affirming that God always delivers on his promises (10:36).

What is the reward of faith? Many of us would respond, "Heaven!" But this is only part of the answer. First and foremost, the reward is the approval and pleasure of God. God says that his soul finds no pleasure in anyone who shrinks back (v. 38; see Habakkuk 2:4 LXX). Yet he promises life to the righteous; he preserves the soul of the faithful (Hebrews 10:38–39). Indeed, God reserves his favor for believers: "For by [faith] the men of old gained approval" (11:2; see vv. 4, 5, 39). In the court of heaven, God testifies on behalf of the faithful and declares them righteous. The one who abandons his or her faith cannot please God (v. 6). The one who holds fast to his or her confidence will receive the greatest reward possible, the commendation of God himself.

This is not to say that the concept of heaven is absent from Hebrews 10–11 (or from the rest of Hebrews, for that matter). The author of Hebrews assures his readers that they own a permanent possession, superior to any physical property (10:34). The Lord promises eternal life to the righteous (10:38). He has prepared a city for them (11:10, 16). The true Promised Land is not the earthly country wherein the patriarchs resided but the heavenly one for which they themselves hope (vv. 14–16). The faithful endure hostility because they look to the reward (v. 26); they may suffer martyrdom to receive a better (that is, eternal) resurrection (v. 35). These illustrations of the ultimate existence of God's people are merely samplings of the rich hope expressed throughout the epistle of Hebrews. The author wants his readers to know that heaven is real, that God resides there, and that someday all believers will be there with him. We pursue a Hebrews 11 faith, because at the end of the journey, we will see God face to face and spend eternity in his presence. What greater reward could there be than that?

NEVER, NEVER, NEVER GIVE UP

The reward, no doubt, inspired the original readers of Hebrews to remain true to Christ—and it ought to do the same for us! When the sinister whisper of Satan tempts us to give up, we must refuse to yield, never surrender. Winston Churchill, in his wartime address at Harrow School, rallied his audience with the following message of hope and resolve: "Never give in. Never give in. Never, never, never, never—in nothing, great or small, large, or petty—never give in except to convictions of honor and good sense. Never yield to force; never yield to the apparently overwhelming might of the enemy." The author of Hebrews offers a similar (and far superior) word of exhortation to the people of God:

> Do not throw away your confidence, which has a great reward. For you have need of endurance, so that when you have done the will of God, you may receive what was promised. For yet in a very little while, he who is coming will come, and will not

delay. But my righteous one shall live by faith; and if he shrinks back, my soul has not pleasure in him. But we are not of those who shrink back to destruction, but of those who have faith to the preserving of the soul. (Hebrews 10:35–39)

God *offers* that reward to everyone; he *gives* it to those who continue in faith. The overarching appeal of Hebrews, then, may be paraphrased as follows: Never give up on Christ! What we have in him is far better than what we have left behind, and the best that he has to offer is yet to come. God-pleasing faith meets trials and temptations with hope and endures to the end.

ASSURANCE AND CONVICTION

The Hebrews writer was confident that his audience possessed God-honoring faith (Hebrews 10:39; see 6:9). He trusted that they looked beyond the physical and temporal to the spiritual and eternal. He describes faith as "the assurance of things hoped for, the conviction of things not seen" (11:1). Faith, then, is the foundation of hope. It makes our reward real and attainable and brings believers through every struggle.

God-pleasing faith is informed, active, and confident: "And without faith it is impossible to please Him, for he who comes to God must believe that He is and that He is a rewarder of those who seek Him" (v. 6). In this passage, the author of Hebrews acknowledges that the existence and character of God are the foundations of Christian faithfulness. From the first verse of the Bible onward, the existence of God is assumed and evidenced (Genesis 1:1). God never came to be, and he will never cease to be. He simply is. Yet, the expression "He is" in Hebrews 11:6 implies far more than just the eternal existence of God. It affirms his personal nature and intimate presence; he is the "I AM" (Exodus 3:14–16). God is a personal God. Hebrews 11:6 notes that God is good and that he rewards those who seek him. That is why the faithful (e.g., Enoch, Abraham, Moses, Jesus) were confident that God would recompense them for their service. They experienced divine grace, and their assurance and conviction grew out of this knowledge of the person, essence, and character of God.

To please God, our faith needs substance. We must come to know God as he really is. When we do, God is pleased with us, and we enjoy assurance and conviction. Indeed, he rewards our faith now and will continue to do so for all eternity.

THE FIRST "HERO" OF HEBREWS 11—YOU AND ME

With these principles of faith in place, the author of Hebrews begins his discussion of the "heroes" of faith (Hebrews 11:3–38). Surprisingly, however, he does not begin with the ancients but with his first-century (and twenty-first century) audience (v. 3). "We" are the first of the faithful: "By faith we understand that the worlds were prepared by the word of God, so that what is seen was not made out of things which are visible" (v. 3). We start where everyone else does, acknowledging God as our Creator. Though no one besides God witnessed the first spark of creation, we *know* that he was there and that he "created the heavens and the earth" (Genesis 1:1). How? By faith! Yet, such faith involves an active response; we come to the Lord, trust him, and seek him diligently (Hebrews 11:6; see Acts 17:24–28; Jeremiah 29:10–14). God rewards this kind of faith.

We can, then, by faith join the ranks of the believing men and women of old who responded to the self-existent, gracious Creator-God and gained his approval (Hebrews 11:2). God wants us to be Hebrews-11 "heroes" of faith.

CONCLUSION

Faith starts and ends with God. It pleases him. It perseveres despite difficulty and assures us of the coming, eternal reward. But faith is not static; it actively seeks God and his will. In the ensuing lessons, we will consider certain aspects of faith as expressed in the lives of the men and women of Hebrews 11. When we follow their example, we, like them, will meet God's approval and receive a reward in heaven.

BIG IDEAS AND APPLICATIONS
- God rewards faith. Hold fast to him, and endure to the end!
- Faith guarantees our hope. Know and trust the Lord!
- We can be "heroes" of faith. Start with God, and imitate the faithful!

SUGGESTED PRAYER

Ask God to help you develop a faith that pleases him. Reaffirm your commitment to the Lord, and if necessary, confess any doubts and sins that have been stifling your spiritual growth.

PERSONAL EXAMINATION

Evaluate the quality of your faith. Do you believe that God is and that he rewards the faithful? Are you consistently drawing near to God and seeking him diligently?

_____

_____

_____

GROUP DISCUSSION

Answer the following questions. Be ready to discuss them as a group.

1. Why did the author of Hebrews write his letter to the Jewish Christians? (Consider the historical background of the epistle. A commentary or handbook on Hebrews may help you with this question.)

_____

_____

2. What does the word *reward* (*misthapodosia*) in Hebrews 10:35 mean? Does this word deny the grace of God? Why, or why not? What reward has God promised believers?

_____

_____

_____

3. What is endurance, and why do believers need it? What are the consequences of giving up on Christ? What helps you persevere when you feel like giving up?

4. Read Hebrews 11:1, 6. How is faith defined in Hebrews 11:1? Is this a comprehensive description of faith? Explain. Why do we need faith, and what does God-pleasing faith believe and do?

5. Read Hebrews 11:3. What do we understand by faith? Why do you think that the author of Hebrews begins his list of believers with "us" and with the creation of the universe?

WEEKLY CHALLENGE

For the next week, be on the lookout for ways God is showing you that he exists and that he is gracious. Record your discoveries in a diary or journal or on your laptop or phone. Be ready to share these findings with the group. If you are not studying these lessons with anyone else, share your discoveries with a family member, friend, or coworker.

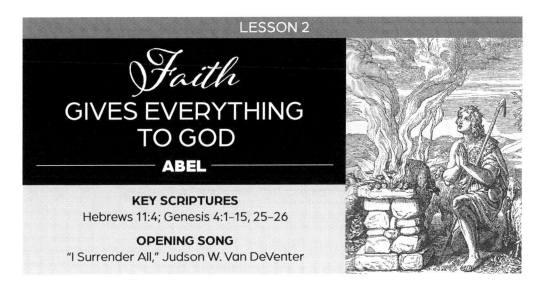

LESSON 2
Faith GIVES EVERYTHING TO GOD
ABEL

KEY SCRIPTURES
Hebrews 11:4; Genesis 4:1–15, 25–26

OPENING SONG
"I Surrender All," Judson W. Van DeVenter

The story of Abel is well known, though the Bible says relatively little about him. He is probably best known as the first murder victim, killed by his own brother Cain. The writer of Hebrews focuses less on this event, however, and more on the faith of Abel—a faith that elicited the jealousy of Cain but found favor in the eyes of God. Because of his faith, Abel willingly sacrificed the best of his possessions to the Lord and died a martyr's death, but he lost nothing of eternal value because God recognized his righteousness and granted him eternal life. Abel gave up "everything" but gained everything. God calls on us to do the same.

AN UNEXPECTED HERO

Genesis 4 records the story of Abel. God had expelled Adam and Eve from the garden of Eden when they conceived and bore their first child Cain (Genesis 4:1). Cain, in Hebrew, means "acquired," and Eve so named him because she recognized that she had *acquired* him with the help of the Lord. As the God-given firstborn, Cain is the anticipated "hero" of the story. But that honor ironically goes to Abel. The record of Abel's birth is not nearly as exciting as Cain's. It is quite mundane: "Again, she gave birth to his brother Abel" (v. 2a). The Bible initially identifies Abel simply as the brother of Cain, and though Genesis 4 does not attach special meaning to the name Abel, the Hebrew root suggests that Abel's life would be "empty" or subject to "sorrow" (BDB, s.v. "הבל"; see Ecclesiastes 1:2; Genesis 50:11). Alternatively, his name may relay an Assyrian root that indicates that he was just another "son" (BDB, s.v. "הבל"). At this point, we would not expect Abel to outshine Cain. Yet, Abel becomes the unlikely "hero" of the story. Why? Because of his faithfulness to God!

A TALE OF TWO SACRIFICES

Cain and Abel became a farmer and a shepherd, respectively. Consequently, they brought offerings to God that were appropriate to their professions, Cain from his crops and Abel from his flocks (Genesis 4:3–4). The Bible does not tell us why they chose to make these offerings; God may have specifically commanded them to do so, or Adam and Eve may have passed the divine tradition down to their sons. Regardless of the specific reason, Cain and Abel intended to express devotion to God with these sacrifices.

Abel offered the best that he had, "the firstlings of his flock and … their fat portions" (v. 4a). This pleased God. Yet, the sacrifice itself seems to have been of secondary importance; God was, first and foremost, pleased with Abel himself: "The Lord had regard for Abel and for his offering" (v. 4b). God wants the heart even more than he wants the sacrifice (1 Samuel 15:22; Proverbs 21:3; Hosea 6:6). That God testifies concerning the offering of Abel says more about Abel than about the gifts themselves (Hebrews 11:4). Abel was a faithful and righteous worshiper of the Lord.

Cain, on the other hand, was rejected not necessarily because he offered the wrong sacrifice but because his character was corrupt. His later interactions with God and Abel clearly evidence a bad heart. After God disregarded his sacrifice, Cain became angry (Genesis 4:5); then, when God exhorted him, he rebelled and murdered his brother (vv. 6–8); when God confronted him again, he lied (vv. 9–10); and when God punished him, he complained (vv. 11–14). Is it any wonder, then, that the Scriptures always speak disapprovingly of Cain (Jude 11; 1 John 3:12)? Why couldn't Cain please God with his offering? He wasn't Abel! (Pardon the pun.) In other words, Cain may have gone through the motions of sacrifice, but his spirit was not engaged in worship. He did not have a heart like Abel.

The writer of Hebrews recognizes the differences between Cain and Abel and their sacrifices and summarizes Abel's faith thus: "By faith Abel offered to God a better sacrifice than Cain, through which he obtained the testimony that he was righteous, God testifying about his gifts, and through faith, though he is dead, he still speaks" (Hebrews 11:4). The sacrifice of Abel was better than that of Cain because Abel offered his by faith. Abel is thus a prime example of the promise of Habakkuk 2:4 and Hebrews 10:38: the righteous live by faith. The faith and gifts of Abel met the favor of God. God therefore declared him to be "Abel the Righteous." In fact, nearly every time the New Testament mentions Abel, it refers to him as "righteous" (Matthew 23:35; Luke 11:51; Hebrews 11:4; 1 John 3:12; cf. Hebrews 12:24).

By faith, Abel continues to speak (Hebrews 11:4). He shows us that loyalty to God always responds with sacrifice. Though we do not offer animals or crops, as Abel and Cain did, we bring gifts to God—our time, our effort, our resources, ourselves. The Macedonian Christians exemplify this kind of giving: "They first gave themselves to the Lord and to us by the will of God" (2 Corinthians 8:5). When we offer ourselves to God, we willingly give him (and others) everything that we possess. We offer holy living, evangelistic outreach, worship, and charity, and if we, like Abel, give them sincerely and faithfully, these gifts bring pleasure to God (1 Peter 2:5; Romans 12:1–2; 15:15–16; Hebrews 13:15–16).

THE HIGH COST OF FAITH

Abel shows us that commitment to God comes with a high price tag. It cost Abel not only his possessions but also his life. The apostle John paraphrases and applies the rest of the story of Cain and Abel as follows: "For this is the message which you have heard from the beginning, that we should love one another; not as Cain, who was of the evil one and slew his brother. And for what reason did he slay him? Because his deeds were evil, and his brother's were righteous. Do not be surprised, brethren, if the world hates you" (1 John 3:11–13). Cain slew his brother because he had allowed Satan to corrupt him and become jealous of Abel. This furthered and (partially) fulfilled the conflict foretold in Genesis 3:15 that there would be hostility between the righteous and the wicked.

The righteous have always endured persecution because of their faith (2 Timothy 3:12). We must ask ourselves, before trials come, *Am I willing to suffer for the cause of Christ? Am I ready to pay the ultimate price?* The apostle Paul, like Abel, shows us what sacrificial commitment to Christ really looks like. At the end of his life, he wrote,

> For I am already being poured out as a drink offering, and the time of my departure has come. I have fought the good fight, I have finished the course, I have kept the faith; in the future there is laid up for me the crown of righteousness, which the Lord, the righteous Judge, will award to me on that day; and not only to me, but also to all who have loved His appearing. (2 Timothy 4:6–8)

We may die for the faith, but pleasing the Lord is worth more than physical life (Philippians 1:12–26; Romans 8:18; 2 Corinthians 4:16–17). If we sacrifice everything, including our lives, for the cause of Christ, we lose nothing of eternal value. Jesus himself affirms that "he who loves his life loses it; and [that] he who hates his life in this world will keep it to life eternal" (John 12:25; see Matthew 16:24–27; Luke 9:23–26; Revelation 2:10; 12:11). The sacrifices that we make here are well worth the losses. Heaven lies before us!

The story of Abel proves another important truth: God is not ignorant of the sacrifices that we make on his behalf. He knows and promises to repay the injustice that we suffer. As we place vengeance in the hands of God, we rest assured that he will (eventually) right all wrongs (2 Thessalonians 1:6–9; Romans 12:17–21; Hebrews 12:24). He did not forget Abel. He will not forget us. We need only to trust in and wait for him.

THE LASTING LEGACY OF ABEL

The writer of Hebrews concludes his discussion of Abel with the following statement: "Through faith, though he is dead, he still speaks" (Hebrews 11:4). Cain (and Satan) could not snuff out faith and righteousness from the earth. Abel's legacy persisted through the line of Seth, that is, through the faithful: "Adam had relations with his wife again; and she gave birth to a son, and named him Seth, for, she said, 'God has appointed me another offspring in place of Abel, for Cain killed him.' To Seth, to him also a son was born; and he called his name Enosh. Then men began to call upon the name of the Lord" (Genesis 4:25–26). Faith presses forward. Worship never ceases. Few may possess faith at any given time, but the enemy cannot eliminate it. In every generation, there are those who believe in the Lord and give themselves to him. Will we wear Abel's mantle of faith? Will we give up everything for the cause of Christ? Will we be an Abel in our generation? If so, the legacy of faith will endure in and through us.

CONCLUSION

Abel may have been a simple shepherd, but his faith was profound. He offered everything to God—the best of his flock and even his own life. He did so by faith. His example speaks to us today. If we listen, we will follow in his footsteps so that it will be said of us that "the Lord had regard for [them] and for [their] offering." Then, we, like Abel, will be righteous and live with God forever.

BIG IDEAS AND APPLICATIONS

- Sincere and sacrificial faith pleases God. Offer your best!
- Faith invites persecution. Be faithful unto death!
- Satan cannot defeat the righteous. Preserve the legacy of faith!

SUGGESTED PRAYER

Praise God that he wants to make you righteous and accept your spiritual sacrifices. Promise him that you will imitate Abel and give up everything for Christ.

PERSONAL EXAMINATION

Have you given everything that you possess—even yourself—to God? What gift(s) can you give him and others this week? Is there anything that you are keeping from him? If so, what, and why?

_____

_____

_____

GROUP DISCUSSION

Answer the following questions. Be ready to discuss them as a group.

1. What did Cain and Abel do for a living? What sacrifices did they offer to God? Why do you think God accepted Abel and his offering, but rejected Cain and his offering?

_____

_____

_____

2. Read 1 Samuel 15:22, Proverbs 21:3, and Hosea 6:6. What might cause God to reject the sacrifices that we offer to him? What can we do to make sure that our gifts please God?

_____

_____

_____

3. Read 1 Peter 2:5, Romans 12:1–2, 15:15–16, and Hebrews 13:15–16. What kinds of sacrifices may we offer today? Can you think of any others? If so, be ready to share your thoughts with the group. (Provide supporting scriptures.)

___

___

___

4. Why did Cain murder his brother Abel? Why should we expect to receive the same (or similar) treatment from wicked people today?

___

___

___

5. What does it mean to give our best to God? Why should we give our best to God? What scriptures encourage you to offer your best? Explain why these passages motivate you.

___

___

___

WEEKLY CHALLENGE

There are a variety of gifts and sacrifices that we can offer to God today—holy living (Romans 12:1–2), sharing the gospel with others (15:15–16), worship (Hebrews 13:15), and helping the needy (v. 16). Choose one of these to give to the Lord this week, give your best, and offer it by faith. If possible, keep what you do a secret. Pay attention to your thoughts and feelings before, during, and after the sacrifice. Share those thoughts and feelings with the Lord in prayer.

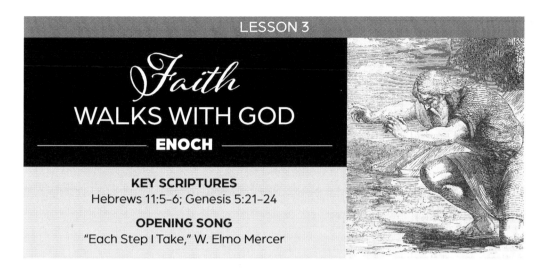

LESSON 3
Faith WALKS WITH GOD
ENOCH

KEY SCRIPTURES
Hebrews 11:5–6; Genesis 5:21–24

OPENING SONG
"Each Step I Take," W. Elmo Mercer

Enoch is a minor character in the Bible, mentioned only once in the Old Testament and a few times in the New Testament (Genesis 5:21–24; Luke 3:37; Hebrews 11:5; Jude 14–15). Enoch was in the seventh generation from Adam. He was the son of Jared and the father of Methuselah. Enoch had a particularly close relationship with the Lord. The Bible summarizes his life in four short verses: "Enoch lived sixty-five years, and became the father of Methuselah. Then Enoch walked with God three hundred years after he became the father of Methuselah, and he had other sons and daughters. So all the days of Enoch were three hundred and sixty-five years. Enoch walked with God; and he was not, for God took him" (Genesis 5:21–24). While this passage follows the same general pattern of the other genealogies in Genesis 5, key differences emphasize the uniqueness of Enoch. Enoch was special in that he was (or became) a man of faith who walked with God.

TOTALLY COMMITTED TO GOD

Genesis 5 implies that Enoch was a man of faith. Hebrews 11 confirms it. The name, lifestyle, and reward of Enoch evidence his commitment to the Lord. The name *Enoch* means "dedicated." The verbal root occurs five times in the Hebrew Bible (Deuteronomy 20:5; 1 Kings 8:63; 2 Chronicles 7:5; Proverbs 22:6) and usually connotes consecration. The corresponding feminine noun means "dedication" and is the source of the name of the Jewish holiday Hanukkah (i.e., the Feast of Dedication). Enoch's name, then, describes well his relationship with the Lord, for Enoch devoted himself to God, held fast to him for most of his earthly life, and walked with him until the end. Only a few characters in the Bible who are specifically described as being men who walked with God. Enoch is the first of these. (Noah and Abraham are the others.) What a special relationship Enoch must have shared with God! He enjoyed daily communion with the Lord and encouraged others to do the same (Jude 14–15). God was pleased with and rewarded Enoch. The end of Enoch's life confirms his faithfulness. Most of us remember Enoch because of his strange exodus from the world, namely that the Lord took him directly to paradise. (Enoch and Elijah are the only individuals in Scripture who escaped the initial sting of death.) God rewarded Enoch's faithfulness with an unending life. Why? Because Enoch walked with him. Enoch dedicated himself to God, but he was (seemingly) not always committed to the Lord. He, like all other believers, had to make the choice to follow the Lord. His loyalty began with repentance.

AN EXAMPLE OF REPENTANCE

The genealogy of Enoch begins the same as the others of Genesis 5, but there is a fascinating shift. (Read Genesis 5:21–24 again.) At sixty-five years old, Enoch became the father of Methuselah, and *then* he resolved to follow God. (For those who are interested in grammar, the Hebrew construction known as the *wayyiqtol* or the *waw consecutive* occurs throughout Genesis 5:21–24. In Hebrew narrative, the *wayyiqtol* frequently describes sequential action. Thus, "Enoch lived … then he begat … then he walked.") Enoch started out going his own way, but then he turned to God and walked with him for the rest of his life. What an example for us today! Sirach 44:16, though not inspired similarly recognizes Enoch's spiritual shift: "Enoch pleased the Lord and was taken up, an example of repentance to all generations" (NRSV). Enoch changed. He chose God. How encouraging to know that we, like Enoch, can repent and get right with the Lord! Enoch is only one example of repentance. The Bible is full of these same kinds of stories. For instance, Manasseh doomed the nation of Judah with his idolatrous practices, but when God chastised him, he turned from his wickedness and received forgiveness (2 Chronicles 33:10–20). Likewise, Paul, initially a violent persecutor of Christians, experienced the grace of God and became one of the most, if not the most, influential evangelist in the history of Christianity (1 Timothy 1:12–16). So, even if failures checker our past, Enoch, Manasseh, and Paul show us that we can turn to God. It is not too late! We can start walking with the Lord now and do so for the rest of our lives (and for all eternity).

TRUST AND REPROVE

What about Enoch changed post-conversion? In other words, what did his walk with God look like? The biblical testimony concerning Enoch suggests that it involved "positive" and "negative" elements, namely (1) trusting God and (2) reproving ungodliness.

Walking with God means trusting God. The author of Hebrews does not specifically mention Enoch's walk with the Lord, but he does highlight the faith that Enoch exercised: "By faith Enoch was taken up so that he would not see death; and he was not found because God took him up; for he obtained the witness that before his being taken up he was pleasing to God" (Hebrews 11:5). Enoch received his reward because he trusted the Lord, but long before God took him, Enoch evidenced his faithfulness by walking with (or living for) God (Hebrews 11:6). Walking with God means walking by faith. The apostle Paul emphasizes the necessity of walking by faith in 2 Corinthians 5:6–9:

> Therefore, being always of good courage, and knowing that while we are at home in the body we are absent from the Lord—for we walk by faith, not by sight—we are

of good courage, I say, and prefer rather to be absent from the body and to be home with the Lord. Therefore we also have as our ambition, whether at home or absent, to be pleasing to him.

In context, Paul equates walking by faith with (1) enduring ill-treatment for the cause of Christ, (2) trusting God to bring us to our eternal home, and (3) living a sanctified life. What's more, Paul practiced what he preached. Enoch did too. So must we! But this is not always easy. In the days of Enoch, the world was spiraling out of control. Immorality, violence, and unbelief were common. The flood was only a few generations away. Still, Enoch chose faith in God. He refused to conform to the world, to satisfy its evil desires. Enoch, in this way, prefigures the teaching of Paul: "But I say, walk by the Spirit, and you will not carry out the desire of the flesh" (Galatians 5:16). If we intend to walk with the Lord, as Enoch did, we must trust that God's will for our lives is always right and best, even if this means walking out of step with the world!

Walking with God also means reproving ungodliness. Reproof was no more desired in the time of Enoch than it is now. As noted above, the world of Enoch was becoming increasingly depraved, and Enoch—the precursor to Noah who also walked with God and preached righteousness (Genesis 6:9; 2 Peter 2:5)—prophesied against the ungodly. Jude reviews the prophetic work of Enoch:

> It was also about these men that Enoch, in the seventh generation from Adam, prophesied, saying, "Behold, the Lord came with many thousands of His holy ones, to execute judgment upon all, and to convict all the ungodly of all their ungodly deeds which they have done in an ungodly way, and of all the harsh things which ungodly sinners have spoken against Him." (Jude 14–15; see Deuteronomy 33:2; 1 Enoch 1:9)

Walking with God requires that we fear God and that we expose the irreverence of those around us (Ephesians 5:11). (The word *godliness* means "piety" or "reverence" toward God!) Living a godly life and preaching against ungodliness often (or always) results in persecution. We need not fear while walking with God, however, for the Lord promises to guard and reward his faithful ones.

Trusting God and reproving ungodliness demand a close relationship with God. Prayer and daily Bible reading/study help us to this end. They draw us close to God and embolden us to teach those around us. Easy? Probably not. Worth it? Absolutely!

STEPPING INTO ETERNITY

Having walked with the Lord for a lifetime, Enoch stepped into eternity with him. God took Enoch directly to paradise, apart from the sting of death. How did God do this? The Bible does not provide the specifics; it simply says that Enoch "disappeared" (Genesis 5:24 NET). The writer of Hebrews does, however, reveal *why* Enoch received his reward: Enoch was faithful to God. The faithfulness of Enoch delighted the Lord, and the Lord rewarded Enoch with eternal life, just as he does all those who diligently seek him (Hebrews 11:5–6). In the same way, God will never disappoint us. If we pledge our allegiance to him, he will see us through physical death and grant us eternal life with him.

CONCLUSION

Faith compels us to traverse the course of this life hand in hand with the Lord, as Enoch did. God was pleased with Enoch because his faith changed him for good. Enoch turned from sin, walked with God, trusted the Lord, reproved ungodliness, and hoped for eternity. When we do the same, we too will please God and walk with him now and forever.

BIG IDEAS AND APPLICATIONS

- Repentance is the first step to God. Turn to him today!
- Walking with God means trusting him and reproving ungodliness. Choose faith, even if you wind up out of step with the wicked majority!
- Paradise awaits the faithful. Seek God daily so that you can walk with him forever!

SUGGESTED PRAYER

Thank God that he gives you the opportunity to walk with him and that he wants you to do so. Ask him to show you how to enjoy an even closer walk with him.

PERSONAL EXAMINATION

Are you communing with God daily, trusting and hoping in him and helping others to know him? Is there anything stifling your relationship with the Lord? What can you do today to draw closer to him?

_____

_____

_____

GROUP DISCUSSION

Answer the following questions. Be ready to discuss them as a group.

1. Read everything the Bible says about Enoch (Genesis 5:21–24; Luke 3:37; Hebrews 11:5; Jude 14–15). What impresses you the most about him?

_____

_____

_____

2. Who in the Bible—besides Enoch—shows you that anyone can repent and begin walking with the Lord? In what way(s) do these examples encourage you to turn to God?

_____

_____

_____

3. What does it mean to walk with God? Find scriptures that speak of walking with God and be ready to share your findings with the group. What can we learn from these passages?

_____
_____
_____

4. How did Enoch's walk with God affect his relationship with others? What can we learn from Enoch's interaction with the ungodly, and how do we apply this to our everyday life?

_____
_____
_____

5. How did God reward Enoch's faithfulness? Why would this have been important to the original readers of Hebrews? Why should this be important to us today?

_____
_____
_____

WEEKLY CHALLENGE

Enoch shows us that faith is not only about making big sacrifices but also about simple, daily fellowship with God. For the next week, plan special times of prayer and Bible study. Stick to your plan as best as you can. Do not, however, avoid spontaneous communication with the Lord. At the end of the week, note how these planned and unplanned times of fellowship helped your walk with God. Be ready to share your experience(s) with the class (or with a friend).

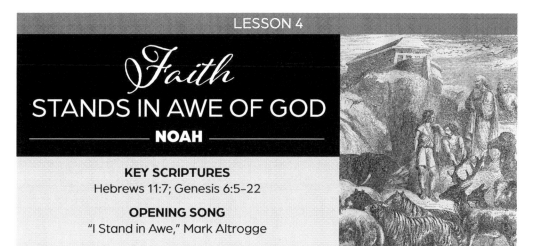

LESSON 4
Faith
STANDS IN AWE OF GOD
NOAH

KEY SCRIPTURES
Hebrews 11:7; Genesis 6:5–22

OPENING SONG
"I Stand in Awe," Mark Altrogge

Let's imagine a world that is totally depraved. The thoughts of every person are only evil continually. Pride and selfishness are the norm, and acts of immorality and violence are ubiquitous. What a terrible place that would be to live! Yet, those were the days of Noah. The world was falling apart, sin was corrupting even those who had been God-worshipers, and humanity was beyond redemption (Genesis 6:1–7, 11–12). Amid that wicked world, however, one man, Noah, was different, favored by God (vv. 8–9; see 7:1). Why? Because he was a man of faith who feared the Lord (Hebrews 11:7).

A TRULY UNIQUE INDIVIDUAL

Noah was the great-grandchild of Enoch, the grandchild of Methuselah, and the son of Lamech (Genesis 5:21–32). Noah's name means "rest." His father so name him because he (Lamech) assumed that he (Noah) would provide *rest* from the divine curse on the land (v. 29; 3:17–19). Although Lamech was correct to assume that his son would play a vital role in the redemption of the world, God used Noah in a way that Lamech probably did not anticipate. (See below.) Noah trusted God and sought a close relationship with him. The Bible specifically says that "Noah found favor in the eyes of the Lord," that he "was a righteous man, blameless in his time," and that he "walked with God" (6:8–9). The Lord looked favorably, that is, graciously and approvingly, on Noah because Noah was a man of character. In contrast, the rest of the world filled God with sorrow and regret (vv. 5–6, 11–12). Noah was not like the people around him. He was righteous and blameless. (Noah is the first man that Scripture identifies as "righteous and blameless.") Noah was not sinless, but he was uniquely loyal to God; and his faith was soon to be tested.

TESTING THE FAITH OF NOAH

Because of the corruption of the world, God determined to cleanse his creation and start over. He gave people 120 years to change (Genesis 6:3). They refused. So, God warned Noah of the coming judgment and commanded him to build an ark (boat) to save himself, his family, and the animals (5:13–21). How did Noah respond to the divine warning and command? He obeyed (6:22). He did not doubt, question, or rebel. He obeyed. Noah still had crops to plant and harvest, a wife to love, and sons to raise, but he obeyed. Though the flood was over a century away and Noah was 480 years old, he did not hesitate. He started building the ark and warning his neighbors of the coming day of judgment (Hebrews 11:7; 1 Peter 3:20; 2 Peter 2:5).

Why did Noah choose obedience in a world that delighted in disobedience? The author of Hebrews says that Noah did so because of his faith in the Lord. The Hebrews writer highlights a particular aspect of Noah's faith—his reverence for God (Hebrews 11:7). Noah obeyed God because he counted the construction of the ark to be an act of worship. Though we do not live in the same world as Noah, we, like Noah, are strangers in a wicked world, waiting for the promised final judgement day. Our faith will be tested, but godly fear will lead us to faithful submission.

REVERENCE AND OBEDIENCE

Hebrews 11:7 summarizes the story of Noah and the flood in this way: "By faith Noah, being warned by God about things not yet seen, in reverence prepared an ark for the salvation of his household, by which he condemned the world, and became an heir of the righteousness which is according to faith." Noah trusted God. So, when God warned him about the future (cf. "things not yet seen," v. 1), Noah responded with reverent obedience. He prepared the ark just as God commanded and according to his specifications (Genesis 6:22; 7:5). Noah's obedience was not partial, careless, or half-hearted. It was complete, focused, and zealous. Faith and (godly) fear are not mutually exclusive. Reverence is, in fact, an indispensable component of faith. Believers must be Godfearers. The translators of the Septuagint, the Greek translation of the Hebrew Bible, recognized this connection between faith and fear, for they sometimes translated the Hebrew word for trust (*ḥāsâ*) with the Greek word for fear (*eulabeomai*; e.g., Proverbs 30:5; Nahum 1:7; Zephaniah 3:12). That same Greek word occurs once in the New Testament—in Hebrews 11:7! The reverence of Noah motivated him to obey God. The author of Hebrews praises Noah for his piety and encourages his readers to imitate Noah (Hebrews 11:7; see 5:7; 12:28).

THE "REWARDS" OF GODLY FEAR

While *ungodly* fear can be debilitating and spiritually disastrous, the Scriptures always connect *godly* fear (reverence) with divine blessing, though the blessings are at times veiled by trial and persecution. In the case of Noah, the writer of Hebrews notes that the faith, reverence, and obedience of Noah yielded the following "rewards": salvation, condemnation, and justification.

Salvation. God saved Noah and his family from the judgment of the world because of their respect for him. He brought them safely through the waters of the flood and protected them within the ark (11:7; see 1 Peter 3:20). But the salvation of Noah was also the salvation of humanity. It was a new beginning! The ancient, noncanonical Jewish work Sirach points out that "Noah was found perfect and righteous; in a time of wrath he kept the race alive; therefore a remnant was left on the earth when the flood came" (44:17 NRSV). The Greek expression rendered "he kept the race alive" literally translates as "he became a substitute." So, during a time of divine wrath, Noah took the place of the wicked world, and God saved a remnant according to the election of grace.

The deliverance of Noah is symbolic of the spiritual rescue that we experience as Christians. Peter writes that "a few, that is, eight souls, were saved through water. There is also an antitype which now saves us—baptism (not the removal of the filth of the flesh, but the answer of a good conscience toward God), through the resurrection of Jesus Christ" (1 Peter 3:20–21 NKJV). Our salvation, like Noah's, begins with water, but it does not end there. As we serve the Lord in reverence and awe, he protects and delivers us from evil and brings us to our eternal home, "the new heavens and the new earth" (Hebrews 12:28; 13:5–6; 2 Peter 3:11–14).

Condemnation. The reverence and obedience of Noah also exposed and condemned the ungodly world in which he lived (Hebrews 11:7). The lexicographer Henry Thayer interprets the meaning of the Greek word translated "condemn" in Hebrews 11:7 (*katakrinō*) as "by one's good behavior to render another's wickedness the more evident and censurable" (Thayer, s.v. "κατακρίνω"; cf. BDAG, s.v. "κατακρίνω"). Noah lived a reverent life and so judged the wicked around him.

But Noah also verbally warned the wicked of the coming judgment in hopes that they would repent (1 Peter 3:18–20; 2 Peter 2:5). He likely endured persecution because of his godly conduct and "judgmental" conversations (2 Timothy 3:12). Still, he did not compromise his convictions. He feared God! In the same way, Jesus commands us to fear God, not man (Matthew 10:28). Oswald Chambers asserts that "the remarkable thing about fearing God is that when you fear God you fear nothing else, whereas if you do not fear God, you fear everything else." Though the world hates us for it, only by living right and exposing wickedness, that is, condemning the world, can we hope to bring others to the Lord (Ephesians 5:11–14; Hebrews 10:23–25).

Justification. Finally, because of his loyalty to God, Noah "became an heir of righteousness which is according to faith" (11:7). Noah was righteous before his faith was tested, but testing confirmed his righteousness. He becomes, then, an example of what it means to be a "righteous one" who "shall live by faith" (10:38; Habakkuk 2:4). Noah walked with God and looked forward to the eternal realm wherein righteousness dwells (Hebrews 1:2; 11:33; 2 Peter 3:11–13). (The heir/inheritance theme occurs throughout Hebrews; see 1:2; 6:17; 9:15.) After the flood, Noah got drunk, uncovered himself, and thus shamed himself and instigated the curse of his son. Noah was not perfect, but he returned to righteousness (Genesis 9:20–27). Righteous people today are likewise subject to failure, but when they fail, they, like Noah, allow godly sorrow to move them to repentance. In this way, Noah now stands justified before God.

The reverent faith of Noah saved him and his family, condemned the wicked world in which he lived, and justified him in the eyes of God. This is the kind of faith that we need—faith that respects God and acts accordingly, faith that always stands in awe of him.

CONCLUSION

Reverence is a necessary component of saving faith. It motivates us to live in conformity with the will of God and prepares us for eternity with him. Like Noah, we will make mistakes, but if we respect God and his word, we will confess our faults and walk with him wherever he goes. God will then shower us with his grace and make us heirs of righteousness (1 John 1:5–10). Noah lived out the conclusion of Ecclesiastes: "Fear God and keep his commandments, for this is the whole duty of man" (Ecclesiastes 12:13 ESV). May we strive to do the same!

BIG IDEAS AND APPLICATIONS

- God-fearers stand out in a wicked world. Let your light shine!
- Reverence motivates obedience. Do what God says!
- God rewards the faithful. Live in the fear of the Lord!

SUGGESTED PRAYER

Praise God for his awe-inspiring character and work. Promise him that you will trust him and grow in your respect for him and his word.

PERSONAL EXAMINATION

How do you show reverence for God? What are some ways in which you have failed to respect God in the past (or in the present)? What will help you to fear God in the future?

GROUP DISCUSSION

Answer the following questions. Be ready to discuss them as a group.

1. Read Genesis 6:1–7, 11–12. Why had the world become so wicked in the days of Noah? Do you think the world is as bad today as it was at that time? Why, or why not?

2. What does the name *Noah* mean? Why did Noah's father give him that name? (Genesis 5:28–29) Read Genesis 6:8–9. How does the Bible describe Noah? Be ready to explain what each of these descriptions mean.

3. When God warned Noah about the coming judgment (flood) and commanded him to build the ark, how did Noah respond, and why? (Hebrews 11:7; Genesis 6:22) What can we learn about the nature of obedience from Noah's response?

4. What is the difference(s) between *godly* fear and *ungodly* fear? (Compare your answer to the description of godly sorrow and worldly sorrow in 2 Corinthians 7:10.) Why is godly fear a necessary component of faith? How can we remove ungodly fear from our hearts and develop godly fear?

5. Hebrews 11:7 suggests that certain "rewards" arise from reverent faith, namely salvation, condemnation, and justification. What did each of these "rewards" look like in the life of Noah? What might these results look like in our lives today?

WEEKLY CHALLENGE

Godliness (reverence) requires spiritual training and sustained effort (1 Timothy 4:6–10). The word of God produces respect for him. Error leads to irreverence. As you read and study your Bible this week, take note of passages that evoke feelings of awe for God, meditate on them, and share them with the group in the next class period. If you are not studying these lessons with a group, discuss your passages with a friend or family member.

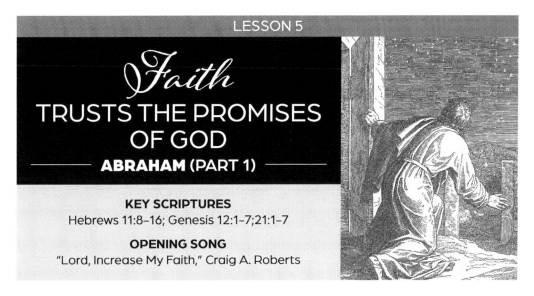

LESSON 5
Faith TRUSTS THE PROMISES OF GOD
ABRAHAM (PART 1)

KEY SCRIPTURES
Hebrews 11:8–16; Genesis 12:1–7; 21:1–7

OPENING SONG
"Lord, Increase My Faith," Craig A. Roberts

Abraham is one of the best-known characters in the Bible. God selected him to be the heir of extraordinary promises and the patriarch of the chosen race (Joshua 24:2; Galatians 3:16; Romans 9:5). Scripture even refers to Abraham as "the friend of God" (Isaiah 41:8; 2 Chronicles 20:7; James 2:23). With that kind of spiritual legacy, we might think that Abraham possessed a super-human faith that is out of our reach. Yet the Scriptures demonstrate that he was a man like us, tried by the same kinds of temptations that beset us. What sets Abraham apart and makes him an example worth following, however, is his unwavering trust in God (Romans 4:20–21). It comes as no surprise, then, that Hebrews 11 devotes more space to Abraham than to any other individual. Consequently, we will discuss the faith of Abraham in this lesson and the next one. We begin with Hebrews 11:8–16, focusing on the so-called land and seed promises.

THE "BLIND" FAITH OF ABRAHAM

Little is known of Abraham's early life. He was probably born in or near Ur of the Chaldeans, in modern-day Iraq, to a pagan family (Joshua 24:14). His birth name, Abram ("exalted father"), likely signifies that his father was wealthy or of noble birth. Abram married Sarai, his half-sister, whom the Scriptures repeatedly describe as a barren woman. His brother Haran died in the city of Ur, and his father Terah died in the city of Haran following the family's migration there (Genesis 11:27–32). The first seventy-five years of Abram's life were thus associated with idolatry, disappointment, and loss. Yet God had bigger and better plans for Abram:

> Now the Lord said to Abram, "Go forth from your country, And from your relatives And from your father's house, To the land which I will show you; And I will make you a great nation, And I will bless you, And make your name great; And so you shall be a blessing; And I will bless those who bless you, And the one who curses you I will curse. And in you all the families of the earth will be blessed." (12:1–3)

We may not fully appreciate the magnitude of God's command to leave Chaldea

(Mesopotamia) because of our modern conveniences (i.e., travel, communication), but God was asking Abram to abandon everything familiar to him—his homeland, his vocation, his relatives—and move to an undisclosed location. (What would you and I do if given such a charge?) Still, when God spoke, Abram listened.

The writer of Hebrews, drawing from the narrative of Genesis, describes Abram's faith in two stages: (1) God called Abram out of Mesopotamia, and Abram obeyed; and (2) Abram sojourned in Canaan and waited on God:

> By faith Abraham, when he was called, obeyed by going out to a place which he was to receive for an inheritance; and he went out, not knowing where he was going. By faith he lived as an alien in the land of promise, as in a foreign land, dwelling in tents with Isaac and Jacob, fellow heirs of the same promise; for he was looking for the city which has foundations, whose architect and builder is God. (Hebrews 11:8–10)

The faith of Abram was, in a sense, blind. Abram did not know where he was going, but he knew whom he was following. He did not know when he (and his heirs) would receive the promises, but he knew that he who had promised was faithful. In fact, Abram was not so much looking for a physical inheritance as he was an eternal one. (More on this later.)

The example of Abram ought to inspire us to trust God. Like Abram, we do not need to have all the answers; we need only to place our confidence in him who knows all things. When we develop a faith like that of Abram, we can step out into the unknown, obey the commands of God, and embark on a great spiritual journey, and as with Abram, an eternal inheritance awaits us at the end of our pilgrimage.

THE "IMPOSSIBLE" HOPE OF ABRAHAM AND SARAH

Belief in God and his promises sometimes raises questions. It did for Abram! God promised Abram not only a land but also a nation of descendants to receive it. Yet Abram had no child of his own. Though Abram never wavered in his trust of God, he at times questioned how God would fulfill these promises (Romans 4:20–21; Genesis 15:2–3).

Abram and Sarai could not have children naturally. Sarai was barren (Genesis 11:30; 16:1). At one time, she even tried to gain an heir for her husband by giving him her maidservant Hagar to be a second wife (Genesis 16:1–16). Ishmael was born to this union but was not the descendent whom God had chosen. God later confirmed his promises to Abram by symbolically changing Abram's name to Abraham ("father of a multitude") and Sarai's to Sarah ("princess"). These name changes demonstrate that God was in control of Abraham's and Sarah's future. Though Abraham and Sarah were by this time too old to conceive a child, God assured them that Sarah would indeed bear a son (Genesis 17:15–22; 18:9–15).

What seems impossible is not too difficult for God. Abraham and Sarah (eventually) believed that they would have a child, and God delivered (18:14). (Pun intended.) Paul thus summarizes the faith of Abraham:

> In hope against hope he believed, so that he might become a father of many nations

according to that which had been spoken, "So shall your descendants be." Without becoming weak in faith he contemplated his own body, now as good as dead since he was about a hundred years old, and the deadness of Sarah's womb; yet, with respect to the promise of God, he did not waver in unbelief but grew strong in faith, giving glory to God, and being fully assured that what God had promised, He was able also to perform. (Romans 4:18–21)

The phrases "as good as dead" and "the deadness of Sarah's womb" indicate that Abraham and Sarah were impotent, but Abraham hoped against hope. The writer of Hebrews echoes the statement in Romans and builds on it:

By faith, even though Sarah herself was barren and he [Abraham] was too old, he received the ability to procreate, because he regarded the one who had given the promise to be trustworthy. So in fact children were fathered by one man—and this one as good as dead—like the number of stars in the sky and like the innumerable grains of sand on the seashore. (Hebrews 11:11–12 NET)

By faith, then, Abraham and Sarah bore Isaac, and the seed of the nation of Israel came into being (Genesis 21:1–7; Romans 9:6–9).

Is it any wonder that Isaiah reminds his audience (and us) to consider the example of Abraham and Sarah and their faith? The prophet declares, "Listen to me, you who pursue righteousness, who seek the LORD: Look to the rock from which you were hewn and to the quarry from which you were dug. Look to Abraham your father and to Sarah who gave birth to you in pain; when he was but one, I called him, then I blessed him and multiplied him" (Isaiah 51:1–2). Though we, like Abraham and Sarah, must sometimes hope against hope, we know that the Lord is trustworthy. God always keeps his promises. We ought, then, to recall often the not-so-impossible hope of Abraham and Sarah and trust God as they did.

THE ULTIMATE GOAL OF THE PATRIARCHS

The writer of Hebrews breaks from his survey of Abraham's life to describe the principal aim of all the patriarchs (Hebrews 11:13–16). They died without receiving the promises, but they died in faith, acknowledging that they were merely "strangers and exiles on the earth" (v. 13). Abraham, Sarah, Isaac, and Jacob did not want a Mesopotamia inheritance, and they did not even really want a residence in Canaan: "They desire a better country, that is, a heavenly one" (v. 16). (Notice the present tense!) Yes, they wanted to see the fulfillment of the physical promises but only insofar as this pointed to the ultimate goal—the heavenly city/country (vv. 10, 16). Oh that our aim would be the same and that our hearts would settle in the place of our true citizenship (13:14; Philippians 3:20–21)!

THE EVERLASTING APPROVAL OF GOD

From the time of the patriarchs onward, God describes himself as "the God of Abraham, the God of Isaac, and the God of Jacob" (e.g., Exodus 3:6; Acts 3:13). The fact that he refers to himself as such demonstrates that "God is not ashamed to be called their God" and that "He has prepared a city for them" (Hebrews 11:16). Abraham longed for an eternal inheritance because his desire was to be forever present with his Lord. Heaven is a place where the faithful will live forever with their God, and that is the greatest blessing anyone can possess.

CONCLUSION

Abraham trusted God. When God promised him a land inheritance, Abraham left everything that he knew. When God promised him and Sarah a son of their own, Abraham wondered but never wavered in unbelief. Abraham, along with Sarah, Isaac, and Jacob, believed that God had prepared something wonderful for them, so they placed their hope in him. We too can rest assured that God will fulfill every promise that he has made to us. We need only to step out in faith and begin the journey.

BIG IDEAS AND APPLICATIONS

- God asks his people to follow him into the unknown. Step out in faith!
- God can do the "impossible." Trust him, his methods, and his timing!
- The aim of believers is to please God. Set your mind on things above!

SUGGESTED PRAYER

Thank God for his great and precious promises. Promise him that you will follow in the footsteps of faithful Abraham, trusting and obeying whatever he (God) has commanded.

PERSONAL EXAMINATION

Which of the promises of God is especially meaningful to you right now? Why? Knowing that God will fulfill his promises, how should you respond? (Be specific.)

___

___

___

GROUP DISCUSSION

Answer the following questions. Be ready to discuss them as a group.

1. What is the first characteristic or event that comes to mind when you think about Abraham? Why is Abraham so important to the Bible story?

___

___

___

___

___

___

2. What does the Bible say about Abraham's early life (e.g., his homeland, his family)? Why did God choose Abraham? (Genesis 18:17–19)

___

3. What did God tell Abraham to do to receive the promises? (Genesis 12:1–3) What promises did God make to Abraham, and how did Abraham respond to them? (Hebrews 11:8–10) What does Abraham's example of obedience teach us about biblical faith?

___

4. What part of the promises of God seemed impossible to Abraham and Sarah? (Genesis 15:2–3; 18:11–12) When God assured them that he could do the "impossible," how did they respond? (Romans 4:18–21; Hebrews 11:11–12)

___

5. What was the ultimate goal of Abraham, Sarah, Isaac, and Jacob, and how do we know that God approved of them? (Hebrews 11:13–16) How did the hope of the patriarchs affect their lives on earth? How can we develop an eternal perspective as they did?

___

WEEKLY CHALLENGE

Faith assures us that God fulfills his "impossible" promises. In the "Personal Examination" section above, you should have thought about a divine promise that is especially meaningful to you right now. For the next seven days, ask God to fulfill that promise. Then wait for him. Watch how he answers. Pay attention to how these daily requests affect your heart. Be ready to share your observations with the group at the next class. If you are not studying these lessons with others, find a close friend with whom you can share your thoughts.

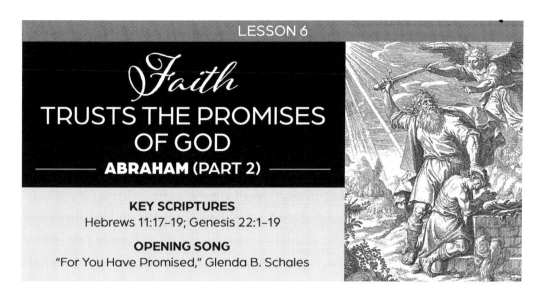

LESSON 6
Faith
TRUSTS THE PROMISES OF GOD
ABRAHAM (PART 2)

KEY SCRIPTURES
Hebrews 11:17–19; Genesis 22:1–19

OPENING SONG
"For You Have Promised," Glenda B. Schales

Abraham was seventy-five years old when he left Haran for the Promised Land. He was one hundred when Isaac was born. The Bible does not reveal how many years passed between Genesis 21 and 22, only that "after these things … God tested Abraham" (Genesis 22:1). Contextual clues suggest that Abraham may have been one hundred twenty-five years old, for Isaac was weaned years before (21:8), conversed with his father and recognized the necessary components of a sacrifice (22:7), made the three-day journey to Moriah, and carried a load on his own (22:4–6). (The Jewish historian Josephus asserts that Isaac was about twenty-five years old; *Jewish Antiquities* 1.227.) So then, Isaac was not a small boy but a young man, the beloved son of his father. This is when Abraham faced his greatest test: God told him to sacrifice Isaac as a burnt offering.

THE ULTIMATE TEST OF FAITH

The command of God was simple but unbelievable: "Take now your son, your only son, whom you love, Isaac, and go to the land of Moriah, and offer him there as a burnt offering on one of the mountains of which I will tell you" (Genesis 22:2). The record tells us that God was testing Abraham, though Abraham was seemingly unaware of this (v. 1). Abraham only knew that God wanted him to kill his son Isaac. The stacking of descriptions ("your son, your only son, whom you love, Isaac") emphasizes the intensity of the command. What thoughts and emotions must Abraham have experienced in this moment! Yet, the Scriptures focus less on Abraham's feelings and more on his response.

Why would God ask Abraham to sacrifice Isaac? Later, in the time of Moses, we learn that human sacrifice is abominable to God, though this is, of course, implied long before the giving of the law (Leviticus 18:21; 20:1–5; Deuteronomy 12:31; 18:9–12; Psalm 106:36–38; Genesis 9:5–6). Was God confused when he told Abraham to kill Isaac, or—worse yet—malevolent? By no means! God did not, in the end, demand Isaac's life, but even if he had, God is not a murderer; he has the right to give life and to take it, and when he does, he does so justly (Job 1:21; 2:10). But what about the promises of God? Did the command to sacrifice Isaac invalidate the faithfulness of God? Not in the mind of Abraham! Still, we may wonder why God would ask him to kill his son.

Again, the command to sacrifice Isaac was a test (Genesis 22:1; Hebrews 11:8). The Hebrew word translated "test" (*nāsâ*) is first used in Genesis 22:1 but is frequently used thereafter of divine testing (Exodus 15:25; 16:4; 20:20; Deuteronomy 8:2, 16; 13:3; 33:8; Judges 2:22; 3:1, 4; 2 Chronicles 32:31; Psalm 26:2). God does not test people because he wants them to fail. He tests them because he wants them to succeed and grow (James 1:2–4, 12–17; 1 Peter 1:6–9). God tested Abraham to prove the quality of his faith and to remove any imperfections in it (Job 23:10; Psalm 66:10; Proverbs 17:3; Zechariah 13:7–9). Abraham passed the test with flying colors because his trust in the promises of God never wavered.

UNWAVERING COMMITMENT TO GOD

Abraham did not hesitate or question God. He was firm in his faith and obeyed. The Bible says, "So Abraham rose early in the morning and saddled his donkey, and took two of his men with him and Isaac his son; and he split wood for the burnt offering, and arose and went to the place of which God had told him" (Genesis 22:3). The distance from Beersheba to Moriah was forty-four miles, a two-day journey in ancient times (v. 4). Abraham marched forward for three days, fully aware that the death of Isaac lay before him. Yet, he did not turn back. And later, when Abraham and Isaac left the servants behind and Isaac asked, "My father! … Behold, the fire and the wood, but where is the lamb for the burnt offering?" Abraham replied simply, "God will provide" (vv. 7–8). Abraham's loyalty to God was limitless.

Why was Abraham so committed? The writer of Hebrews affirms that it was because Abraham was a man of faith:

> By faith Abraham, when he was tested, offered up Isaac, and he who had received the promises was offering up his only begotten son; it was he to whom it was said, "In Isaac your descendants shall be called." He considered that God is able to raise people even from the dead, from which he also received him back as a type. (Hebrews 11:17–19)

Abraham trusted the promises of God, including the part about Isaac being the heir (Genesis 17:19, 21; 21:12). While he did not know exactly how God would fulfill his promises concerning Isaac, Abraham knew that he would.

The conviction of Abraham is manifested in Genesis 22:5. After coming to the land of Moriah, Abraham saw the mountain where he was to sacrifice Isaac and said to his servants, "Stay here with the donkey; the lad and I will go yonder and worship, and we will come back to you" (NKJV). The pronoun used in the final clause is significant; Abraham did not say "*I* will come back to you," but "*we* will come back to you." Abraham was convinced that Isaac would survive the sacrifice. The writer of Hebrews tells us what Abraham was thinking. Though there is no biblical record of resurrection before the time of Abraham, the patriarch believed that God had the power to raise Isaac from the dead (Hebrews 11:19; see vv. 11–12). Abraham was mistaken in his estimation of how God would preserve Isaac, but he never wavered in unbelief.

Abraham had, as it were, already offered Isaac to God. (The Greek perfect tense in Hebrews 11:17 may suggest that the sacrifice was as good as done in the heart of Abraham.) Not even Isaac would come between Abraham and God. Richard Taylor observes that "Abraham surmounted this trial because Isaac had never become an idol." The offering of Isaac was the climactic point and the surest proof of Abraham's faith. His love for God motivated him to obey the command and so prove his faith (The ancient yet uninspired works of Philo and the Apocrypha provide insightful commentary on the testing of Abraham and his motivation to obey God. See Philo, *On the Life of Abraham* 167, 170; Sirach 44:19–20; 1 Maccabees 2:52. These passages are available for free online.) No wonder the angel of the Lord responded to Abraham's obedience, "Now I know that you fear God, since you have not withheld your son, your only son, from Me" (Genesis 22:12). For Abraham, there was no way to separate faith from obedience. So then, James could rightly say,

> Was not Abraham our father justified by works when he offered up Isaac his son on the altar? You see that faith was working with his works, and as a result of the works, faith was perfected; and the Scripture was fulfilled which says, "Abraham believed God, and it was reckoned to him as righteousness," and he was called the friend of God. You see that a man is justified by works and not by faith alone. (James 2:21–24)

Abraham believed and obeyed because he was totally committed to his Lord.

DIVINE TRUSTWORTHINESS

When Abraham and Isaac reached the designated place for the offering, Abraham built an altar, arranged the wood, bound his son, laid him on the altar, and raised the knife. But God stopped him from killing Isaac (Genesis 22:9–11). The Lord honored the faith of Abraham, provided a substitute sacrifice, and reaffirmed his covenant promises (vv. 12–18). Abraham assumed that God would raise Isaac from the dead; God fulfilled his promise another way and thus showed himself to be faithful and gracious.

A SYMBOL FOR THE FUTURE

The writer of Hebrews suggests that the "death" and "resurrection" of Isaac was symbolic (Hebrews 11:19; see 9:8–9). While the expression "[Abraham] also received [Isaac] back as a type" does not necessarily mean that the offering of Isaac is a portrait of Christ, the overall picture of the story envisions the New Testament sacrifice. Just as Abraham offered his one and only, beloved son on the mountain where Jerusalem would later be established, so God provided the sacrifice of his one and only, beloved son Jesus (2 Chronicles 3:1; John 3:16). What God did *not* make Abraham do, he did himself to prove that he is the Lord who provides (YHWH Yireh; Genesis 22:14). Thank God that we can be a part of the divine promises made to Abraham, fulfilled in Jesus Christ!

CONCLUSION

Abraham trusted the promises of God. When tested, his faith never wavered. He trusted and obeyed God, and God provided the sacrifice. The Lord calls us to follow in the footsteps of believing Abraham (Galatians 3:6–9, 26–29). God always keeps his promises. He even provides our sacrifice, Jesus Christ. When we trust him, as Abraham did, he gives us all things in Christ (2 Corinthians 1:20; Ephesians 1:3).

BIG IDEAS AND APPLICATIONS

- God tests the faith of his people. Trust him in the trial!
- God is trustworthy. Give him everything that you have!
- Jesus is the sacrificial lamb of God. Thank God for his grace!

SUGGESTED PRAYER

Praise God for his faithfulness. Promise him that you will put your trust in him and in his promises, especially during times of testing. Thank God for his gracious pardon and providence in Christ Jesus.

PERSONAL EXAMINATION

What thoughts and feelings do you typically experience when your faith is tested? Does God want you to respond the way that you normally do? What helps you to trust God and his promises?

_____

_____

_____

GROUP DISCUSSION

Answer the following questions. Be ready to discuss them as a group.

1. Why would God's command to sacrifice Isaac have been especially difficult for Abraham to hear and obey? How do you think you would respond if God asked you to kill your child (or someone else whom you love)? Explain.

_____

_____

_____

_____

_____

2. What does the Bible mean when it says that God tests people but that he does not tempt people (James 1:2–8, 12–17)? How does God test people, and why?

3. When God commanded Abraham to kill Isaac, how did he (Abraham) respond? Why did Abraham respond the way he did? Does the Bible separate faith and obedience? Explain.

4. What do we learn about the character of Abraham from his willingness to offer Isaac as a burnt offering? What did God promise to do for Abraham because of his obedience? (Genesis 22:15–18) What do we learn about the character of God from this story?

5. What similarities do you see in the sacrifices of Isaac and Jesus? In what way(s) do these similarities bolster your faith?

WEEKLY CHALLENGE

God sometimes demands "big" sacrifices, allowing difficulties to come into our lives to test the quality of our faith. Is there something God has asked you to do that you have not yet obeyed? Are you facing a particularly trying circumstance right now? Meditate on the promises of God. Choose to obey the Lord this week. See what happens. Be ready to share your experience with the group or with someone whom you trust.

LESSON 7
Faith SUBMITS TO GOD
ISAAC AND JACOB

KEY SCRIPTURES
Hebrews 11:20–21; Genesis 27:1–40; 47:29–48:22

OPENING SONG
"Have Thine Own Way, Lord," Adelaide A. Pollard

Throughout the Old and New Testaments, the Lord identifies himself as "the God of Abraham, the God of Isaac, and the God of Jacob" (e.g., Exodus 3:6; Acts 3:13). The writer of Hebrews affirms that "God is not ashamed to be called their God" (Hebrews 11:16). Though Abraham was by no means perfect, we see why God chose him; Isaac and Jacob, on the other hand, we might consider surprising additions. Isaac was, at times, passive and even carnal, and Jacob started out deceitful and self-centered. Still, God worked with and on both men to accomplish his purpose so that by faith they might bless others and worship him (vv. 20–21).

THE SUBMISSIVENESS AND SENSUALITY OF ISAAC

The story of Isaac is a mixture of virtue and vice, a tragic tale of a privileged man who drifted into self-indulgence. Isaac had everything going for him. He was the miracle child of Abraham and Sarah; his father served God and instructed him (Isaac) to do the same (Genesis 18:19); God himself arranged the marriage of Isaac and Rebekah and providentially protected him from his enemies. But "Isaac [seems to have been] comfortable to let life happen to him rather than to make life happen" (Daniel Lockwood). He was, at times, passive to a fault. (See below.)

The submissiveness—not the passivity—of Isaac is commendable. For instance, when Abraham took him to the mountain of sacrifice, Isaac did not object (22:9); when he and his wife Rebekah could not have children of their own, he prayed to God (25:21); and when the Philistines threatened him, Isaac sought a peaceable solution (26:15–22). Sadly, however, the passivity of Isaac eventually deteriorated into sensuality—especially in his old age.

Isaac played favorites with his sons Esau and Jacob. The Bible says that "Isaac loved Esau … but Rebekah loved Jacob" (25:28). Why did Isaac love Esau more than Jacob? Because Esau made tasty food! The Scriptures inform us that Esau was "a man who knew hunting/game" and that Isaac loved Esau "because of the game in his mouth" (vv. 27–28, literal translation). The Hebrew word translated "game" (*sayid*) and its complement "tasty food" (*matʿām*) are key terms in the story of Isaac. Of the nineteen occurrences of *sayid* in the Old Testament, ten are associated with Isaac (25:27, 28; 27:3, 5, 7, 19, 25, 30, 31, 33). Likewise, *mat'ām* is used almost exclusively of Isaac (27:4, 7, 9, 14, 17, 31; cf. Proverbs 23:3, 6). This focus on food suggests that late in life Isaac became overly concerned with what felt (or tasted) good, rather than what was good.

The sensuality of Isaac is obvious from the record of Jacob stealing the patriarchal blessing. Isaac was old and nearly blind, and he (incorrectly) assumed that he was close to death; so, he sought to bless his favorite son Esau (Genesis 27:1). During the patriarchal age, the blessed child carried the family legacy and led the clan. But Esau did not deserve this blessing; he was a foolish and profane man who sold his birthright and married pagan women (25:29–34; 26:34–35; Hebrews 12:16–17). God had revealed to Rebekah that Jacob would be the heir of the divine blessing (Genesis 25:22–23). (Isaac may not have known of this divine prediction, but the flow of the story suggests that he did.) Still, Isaac wanted to bless Esau, instead of Jacob, not because Esau was worthy but because he made tasty food.

THE VIRTUE OF ISAAC

The future hanging in the balance, Rebekah and Jacob hatched a plan to deceive Isaac and seize the patriarchal blessing. God, no doubt, disapproved of their dishonesty, but he was still able to accomplish his purpose, that is, the blessing of Jacob, through their sinful choices. And to Isaac's credit, "when he … learned of [his] mistake [of blessing Jacob instead of Esau], he refused to change it. Apparently, he recognized God's providential hand in the events of that day" (Daniel King, Sr.). Isaac then assigned another (inferior) blessing to his son Esau. Why? Because he determined to trust God and submit to his will.

Faith moved Isaac to virtue. Isaac rejected his own desires, accepted the plan of God, and moved the story of redemption forward: "This blessing of Isaac had the wondrous power of shaping and controlling the future of his posterity, because in virtue of his faith, his mind and will had become one with the mind and will of God himself" (Franz Delitzsch). The author of Hebrews highlights this future-looking faith of Isaac: "By faith Isaac blessed Jacob and Esau, even regarding things to come" (Hebrews 11:20). Isaac initially wanted to bless Esau because of his misguided, sensual desires, but he eventually changed his mind, trusted God, and blessed his sons in accordance with divine revelation. Like Isaac, we too must learn to deny ourselves, trust God's purpose, and bless the lives of others (Luke 9:23; Romans 13:14; Philippians 2:3).

THE DISHONESTY AND GREED OF JACOB

Jacob was the culturally disadvantaged second-born son of Isaac and Rebekah. His second-class status, along with the partial love of his father, led Jacob to envy his older twin brother Esau, resulting in a long-standing, lamentable conflict between them. In fact, the siblings had even fought in the womb (Genesis 25:22). At the time of their birth, Jacob got his name because he was clinging to Esau's heel. The name *Jacob* corresponds to the Hebrew word for "heel" (*'āqēb*), indicating that Jacob was a "heel-grabber," that is, "supplanter" or "deceiver" (v. 26). Sadly, Jacob lived up to his name. He deceived his brother and his father and claimed the right and blessing of the firstborn (vv. 29–34; 27:5–40).

Having stolen the birthright and the blessing from Esau, Jacob fled for his life to the East (27:41–28:5). There he lived with his uncle Laban, fell in love with Laban's daughter Rachel, and worked for seven years to marry her (29:18–20). Yet at the time of the wedding, the trickster got a taste of his own medicine; Laban tricked him into marrying the firstborn Leah before Rachel and repeatedly changed Jacob's wages thereafter (vv. 21–30; 31:7–8, 41). Consequently, Jacob broke company with Laban and returned to Canaan with his wives, children, and possessions.

On the way to his homeland, Jacob had one final confrontation with Laban. God intervened on Jacob's behalf, protecting him from the wrath of his father-in-law. Jacob thereafter returned to Canaan, reconciled with his brother Esau, and settled his family. What a surprisingly "happy ending" for the swindler Jacob! But this "happy ending" was the result of a lifelong transformation, directed by God himself. (In reality, Jacob continued to experience conflict—between his wives and his sons—until the "happy ending" in Egypt. We will discuss this further in Lesson 8.)

THE TRANSFORMATION OF JACOB

God changed Jacob. He taught him to appreciate that he (God) was the source of blessing and that he alone was the only rightful recipient of worship. Moving through the life of Jacob, we can see a transformation. Jacob learned valuable spiritual lessons in the following locations: Bethel, Haran, Gilead, Mahanaim, Peniel (or Penuel), Shechem, and Beersheba. (Some of the points in the next paragraph come from Daniel Lockwood.)

At *Bethel*, the place where he first met the Lord, Jacob promised to serve God, if he would protect him (Genesis 28:10–22). At *Haran*, Jacob learned how it feels to be deceived (29:1–31:21). In *Gilead*, he sealed a covenant with Laban in the name of God (31:43–55). At *Mahanaim*, the angels of God met Jacob and reassured him that God was with him and would be with him when he met his brother (32:1–2). At *Peniel* (or *Penuel*), the climactic event in Jacob's transformation occurred; he wrestled with God himself (32:22–32; cf. Hosea 12:2–4); there Jacob finally came to accept the sovereignty of God and the importance of faith; God therefore changed his name to Israel ("he struggles with God"); Jacob learned that the conflicts that he had experienced with others throughout his lifetime were merely symptoms of his struggle with God. The fight at *Peniel* humbled Jacob and thereby resulted in a blessing from God. At *Shechem*, just before returning to Bethel, Jacob worshiped God and removed every form of idolatry from his camp (Genesis 33:18–20; 35:1–4). At *Bethel*, God reaffirmed his covenant with Jacob, and Jacob built an altar to God (35:6–15). Years later, Jacob fashioned his last-recorded altar in *Beersheba* and migrated to Egypt, trusting that God would fulfill his promises when he returned his (Jacob's) descendants to Canaan (46:1–4).

By the end of his life, Jacob was a man of faith. The author of Hebrews highlights the final response of Jacob's faith—his blessing of Ephraim and Manasseh and his worship of God: "By faith Jacob, as he was dying, blessed each of the sons of Joseph, and worshiped, leaning on the top of his staff" (Hebrews 11:21; see Genesis 47:29–31; 48:1–22). Jacob made a complete turnaround. No longer was he grabbing blessings; he was giving them (48:1–49:33). No longer was he striving against God; he was serving and worshiping him. When we, like Jacob, allow the Lord to change us from the inside out, we too will submit to the will of God, blessing others and worshiping the Lord.

CONCLUSION

The overlapping stories of Isaac and Jacob show that faith changes people, leads them to submit to the will of God, and results in blessing and worship. The patriarchs failed in many ways, but they were (or became) men of faith. Isaac and Jacob moved in different directions. Isaac became more self-focused, and Jacob more God-focused, but both finished strong. We too can become spiritual victors, when we recognize God's providence, respond in faith, submit to his will, and allow him to transform us from the inside out.

BIG IDEAS AND APPLICATIONS

- Submission to God requires trust and obedience. Learn and do his will!
- God wants to change us from the inside out. Accept his gracious instruction!
- Faith results in worship and blessing. Find ways to show your love for God and for others!

SUGGESTED PRAYER

Thank God for the changes that he has effected in you and for the blessings that he has given to you. Promise him that you will respond in worship. Ask God to give you opportunities to bless others.

PERSONAL EXAMINATION

Do you ever struggle with sensuality (Isaac) or selfishness (Jacob)? What has God done to change you so that you can overcome this temptation(s)? How should you respond, and why?

GROUP DISCUSSION

Answer the following questions. Be ready to discuss them as a group.

1. Was the submissive (passive) character of Isaac a virtue or a vice (or both)? Explain. Why did Isaac love Esau more than Jacob? What does his reason(s) for loving Esau more than Jacob say about Isaac, and what did it tempt him to do?

2. According to Hebrews 11:20, what did Isaac do by faith? Why was faith needed to perform this act? How can we apply the example of Isaac?

3. What does the name *Jacob* mean, and in what way(s) did Jacob live up to his name? Does it surprise you that God chose Jacob to be the heir of the promise(s) and the namesake of the nation of Israel? Why, or why not?

4. Summarize the spiritual transformation of Jacob. (Include what God did to Jacob to change him and what changes we see in Jacob from the beginning of his life to the end.) In what way(s) does the transformation of Jacob encourage you?

5. According to Hebrews 11:21, what did Jacob do by faith? What deeds of Jacob demonstrate a spiritual transformation? How can we apply the example of Jacob?

WEEKLY CHALLENGE

God transforms us so that we will bless others and worship him, but we must submit to his will. Look for opportunities to do good to others and to praise God. You do not have to share what you did with the group next week but be ready to describe how these experiences affected you. If you are not studying with a group, write down your experiences in a personal journal or diary for subsequent reflection.

LESSON 8
Faith HOPES IN GOD
— JOSEPH —

KEY SCRIPTURES
Hebrews 11:22; Genesis 50:15–26

OPENING SONG
"Jesus, Draw Me Ever Nearer," Margaret Becker

The patriarchs are a hodgepodge of noble and shameful traits, but their trust in God often tempers and redeems their failures. Amid this collection of characters is a unique, shining example of faith—Joseph. Joseph is a fascinating individual. Though he was by no means sinless, his character seems to have been free of any major defect, his decisions were God-centered, and his faith was pure. There is much to learn from Joseph, but the writer of Hebrews emphasizes a particular aspect—Joseph's forward-looking, hopeful belief in God. Indeed, hope is the defining characteristic of his faith; it characterizes his outlook from beginning to end. Joseph knew God was in control, and he accepted whatever God sent his way.

A DYSFUNCTIONAL FAMILY

Joseph was born to a family fraught with conflict: "To say Joseph faced the obstacle of a dysfunctional family is an understatement" (Daniel Lockwood). His mother Rachel and her sister Leah competed for the love of his father Jacob, and Jacob played favorites with his wives and with his sons and loved Rachel and Joseph more than any of the others. Accordingly, the brothers of Joseph could not stand him. So, when Joseph reported their wickedness to Jacob, the conflict only worsened (Genesis 37:2). This feud came to a head when Jacob gave Joseph a special, long-sleeved robe as a gift (vv. 3–4).

God even communicated directly with Joseph in dreams. Elated that God had spoken to him, Joseph told his brothers and his father about his dreams, predicting his eventual rule over the family (vv. 5–11). This was the last straw for his brothers. "They hated him even more for his dreams and for his words. … His brothers were jealous of him" (vv. 8, 11). So, when Jacob sent Joseph to check on the brothers as they were pasturing the flocks, they plotted against him (Joseph). "Here comes this dreamer!" they said, "Now then, come and let us kill him and throw him in one of the pits" (vv. 19–20; see 42:21). However, they did not kill him. Led by Judah, they decided to sell Joseph to slave traders (37:21–28). They even found a way to cover up their crime; they stripped Joseph of his robe, dipped it in goat's blood, and took it to their father (vv. 29–35). Overcome by emotion, their father assumed the worst, that a wild animal had killed his beloved son Joseph. "Meanwhile, the Midianites sold [Joseph] in Egypt to Potiphar, Pharaoh's officer, the captain of the bodyguard" (v. 36). Nonetheless, Joseph remained loyal to God, God never abandoned him, and Joseph refused to slip into a victim mentality.

Joseph teaches us that God can use the good and the bad of our upbringing to grow our faith and accomplish good in the future. Whether our family is functional or dysfunctional, we can trust God, the perfect father, to love and provide for us. Our physical families show us—for better or for worse—what it means to be a part of a spiritual family. We, like Joseph, must remember that our heavenly father holds our future in his hands.

TERRIBLE CIRCUMSTANCES, UNCOMPROMISING INTEGRITY

Alone in a foreign land, Joseph continued to respect the sovereignty of God. He did not compromise his morals or give up on life. As a slave in the house of Potiphar, Joseph worked hard, and God blessed him—and Potiphar noticed (Genesis 39:1–6)! Joseph was also a handsome man—and Potiphar's wife noticed (vv. 6–7)! A major test was coming Joseph's way.

The wife of his master, undoubtedly a powerful and attractive woman, tried to seduce Joseph into an affair. She brazenly and repeatedly enticed him, "Lie with me," but Joseph always refused (vv. 7, 10). Joseph's answer to her enticement manifests his integrity: "Behold, with me here, my master does not concern himself with anything in the house, and he has put all that he owns in my charge. There is no one greater in this house than I, and he has withheld nothing from me except you, because you are his wife. How then could I do this great evil and sin against God?" (vv. 8–9). Joseph knew adultery was a sin against Potiphar and ultimately against God, so he refused to cave to lust; he literally fled from fornication (vv. 11–18; see 2 Corinthians 6:18). The consequence? Potiphar's wife falsely accused him of rape, and Potiphar imprisoned him (Genesis 39:19–20). Still, Joseph continued to entrust himself, his present, and his future to God.

In prison, rather than wallow in self-pity, Joseph endured the injustice. He knew that God was with him, and again God blessed him (vv. 21–23). God, at last, provided Joseph a way out of prison—or so it would seem—when the pharaoh imprisoned his cupbearer and his baker (40:1–4). The cupbearer and the baker had prophetic dreams, which Joseph miraculously interpreted; Joseph predicted that Pharaoh would release the cupbearer and behead the baker (vv. 5–22). The only request Joseph made of the cupbearer was that after his release he would try to exonerate him (vv. 14–15). Sadly, "the chief cupbearer did not remember Joseph, but forgot him" (v. 23). God thus kept Joseph in jail for a couple more years. From this experience, Joseph, no doubt, learned perseverance and trust.

Finally, deliverance came. God caused Pharaoh to dream about a severe drought that was on its way to Egypt (and the surrounding regions), and the cupbearer remembered Joseph (41:1–13). Pharaoh summoned Joseph, Joseph interpreted Pharaoh's dreams, and Pharaoh commissioned Joseph to prepare Egypt for the famine (vv. 14–49). The king gave Asenath, the daughter of an Egyptian priest, to be the wife of Joseph (v. 50), and Joseph honored God and his providence by naming his children Manasseh ("God has made me forget all my trouble and all my father's household," v. 51) and Ephraim ("God has made me fruitful in the land of my affliction," v. 52).

When the famine struck, Joseph's brothers came to Egypt to buy grain (42:1–5). Instead of exacting revenge, however, Joseph tested them to see if they had changed (42:6–44:34). When they passed his trials, he revealed his identity and invited the whole Israelite clan to live with him in Egypt (45:1–47:12). Joseph never punished his brothers, even after the death of their father; he assured them: "Do not be afraid, for am I in God's place? As for you, you meant evil against me, but God meant it for good in order to bring about this present result, to preserve many people alive. So therefore, do not be afraid; I will provide for you and your little ones" (50:19–21). Faith prepared Joseph to forego vengeance and choose love instead of hate. Oh that we would follow his example, persevering through trial and giving God the glory, regardless of our circumstances!

WHERE FAITH AND PROVIDENCE INTERSECT

Joseph endured hostility, overcame immorality, learned patience, and dismissed revenge because he trusted God to right all the wrongs and to solve all the problems in his own time and in his own way. Joseph did not whitewash a bad situation, but his hope was bigger than his difficulties. He knew that God was with him regardless of the circumstances. Genesis 39 emphatically repeats the phrase "the LORD was with Joseph," indicating that in everything the providence of God was active in the life of Joseph (vv. 2, 3, 21, 23). Similarly, when we acknowledge that God is with us and working in our lives, we can endure the worst that Satan throws our way. Why? Because we, like Joseph, know that the best is yet to come (Romans 8:18, 28). We may suffer terrible injustice, we may have to wait longer than we would prefer before our deliverance comes, but faith sustains our hope and empowers us to persevere.

LOOKING TO THE FUTURE

The writer of Hebrews draws attention to a single act of faith at the end of the Joseph's life: "By faith Joseph, when he was dying, made mention of the exodus of the sons of Israel, and gave orders concerning his bones" (Hebrews 11:22; see Genesis 50:22–26). Joseph knew that God would eventually bring the Israelites out of Egypt; this knowledge was likely based on secondhand information, that is, Joseph learned of the coming exodus from his father who had heard about it from God (Genesis 48:3–4, 21–22; see 15:13–16; 46:2–4). But the faith of Joseph was no less real or solid, the promise of God being its foundation.

Joseph faced death trusting that one day he and his people would inherit the promised land. When the Israelites departed from Egypt decades later, they took the bones of Joseph and buried them in Canaan (Exodus 13:19; Joshua 24:32). Joseph, like the other patriarchs, believed that God would fulfill his promises and that these promises were not limited to the here-and-now. As we put our trust in the Lord, we also eagerly anticipate the realization of the promise of God, namely our eternal abode with God in the true promised land.

CONCLUSION

Joseph was a man who faced awful circumstances, none of which were his own fault, but he never blamed God or tried to avenge himself. He trusted that God was in control and that he (God) would keep his promises to his people. Joseph's hope in God permitted him to persevere. As we develop this same kind of forward-looking faith, we can face whatever comes, knowing that God is with us and that our promised land lies before us.

BIG IDEAS AND APPLICATIONS
- Hope motivates purity. Remain true to the Lord, regardless of your situation!
- The presence of God empowers his people to persevere. Know that God is with you!
- Faith looks to future. Hasten the coming of Christ and the fulfillment of his promises!

SUGGESTED PRAYER

Thank God that he redeems our past and gives us a future. Promise him that you will trust in his continued providence, regardless of your present circumstances. Ask him to come again soon and bring you home to be with him forever. (Regarding this final request, consider Titus 2:13 and 2 Peter 3:12.)

PERSONAL EXAMINATION

Do you look to the future with joy or fear? Why? What can you learn from Joseph that will help you to have a hopeful faith, and how will you put those principles into practice?

_____

_____

GROUP DISCUSSION

_____

_____

_____

Answer the following questions. Be ready to discuss them as a group.

1. Describe the family dynamics of Jacob's home. Compare the attitudes and actions of Joseph with those of his brothers. Why do you think Joseph turned out so good and his brothers so bad, even though they grew up in the same household?

2. Why do you think Joseph refused to succumb to victimhood? Why do we sometimes allow ourselves to feel like a victim? How can we develop a victorious spirit?

3. Why did God allow Joseph to face injustices? How might Joseph personally benefit from his experiences? How did others benefit? (Genesis 50:20)

4. Read Romans 8:18–39. How does this scripture help you endure affliction?

5. According to Hebrews 11:22, what did Joseph do by faith? How does the hope of Joseph parallel the Christian hope? How does hope carry you through life and prepare you to face death?

WEEKLY CHALLENGE

Jürgen Moltmann allegedly wrote, "Totally without hope one cannot live. To live without hope is to cease to live." Too many people in the world today "live" without hope, separated from Christ. This week find someone who is hurting (a Christian or a non-Christian) and show him or her the love of Jesus through a kind word or deed. Try to give him or her a sense of hope. If possible, keep this interaction between you, this person, and God.

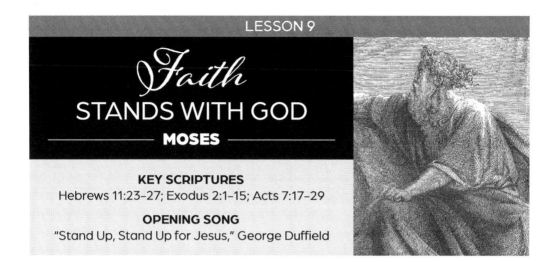

LESSON 9
Faith STANDS WITH GOD
MOSES

KEY SCRIPTURES
Hebrews 11:23–27; Exodus 2:1–15; Acts 7:17–29

OPENING SONG
"Stand Up, Stand Up for Jesus," George Duffield

Charles Swindoll tells the story of an older woman who studied the life of Moses so thoroughly that she would tell others, "I know Moses so well that to me he doesn't even look like Charlton Heston anymore." Charlton Heston may have been the face of Moses for a generation, but the actor was no Moses. Moses is a giant of a character in Scripture and particularly in Hebrews. The writer of Hebrews mentions Moses several times and allocates nearly as much space to him as to Abraham (Hebrews 3:2–3, 5, 16; 7:14; 8:5; 9:19; 10:28; 11:23–28). Moses was the spiritual leader who led the Israelites out of Egypt and gave them the law. He proved to be a faithful servant of God. But how did Moses demonstrate his faithfulness? We will consider the life of Moses in this lesson and the next one, but in this study, we will focus on his allegiance to God and Israel.

A SPECIAL CHILD AND HOPEFUL PARENTS

The first act of faith associated with Moses in Hebrews 11 is performed not by Moses but by his parents Amram and Jochebed (Exodus 2:1; 6:20): "By faith Moses, when he was born, was hidden for three months by his parents, because they saw he was a beautiful child; and they were not afraid of the king's edict" (Hebrews 11:23; see Exodus 2:2). The king of Egypt, frightened by the strength of the resident nation of Israel, ordered the murder of every newborn Hebrew male (1:22). Amram and Jochebed made a courageous choice; they disobeyed Pharaoh and hid their baby boy. Because of his beauty, the parents of Moses believed God would use this child in some way to save his people. (David McClister notes that "a handsome appearance was considered a sign of divine favor." Cf. Acts 7:20 and Philo, *On the Life of Moses* 1.9.)

Amram and Jochebed defied the king because they trusted in God (Hebrews 11:23; see Matthew 22:21). When they could no longer hide the infant, they placed him where Pharaoh's daughter would find him, trusting that God would see to the protection of Moses and prepare him for the task of delivering the Israelites (Exodus 2:3–10; Acts 7:21–22). In this way, God providentially saved Moses from death. Jochebed was even allowed to nurse him and instruct him during his formative years, no doubt, telling him of his heritage and his responsibility toward God. Still, Moses grew up in the house of

Pharaoh (v. 23). After years of Hebrew and Egyptian education, would he choose what was easy or what was right? Would he stand with God and Israel or with Pharaoh and Egypt?

CHOOSING GOD AND HIS PEOPLE

Moses made a hard decision. He chose to align himself with the Lord and with his people. The author of Hebrews writes, "By faith Moses, when he was grown up, refused to be called the son of Pharaoh's daughter, choosing rather to endure ill-treatment with the people of God than to enjoy the passing pleasures of sin, considering the reproach of Christ greater riches than the treasures of Egypt; for he was looking to the reward" (Hebrews 11:24–26; see Exodus 2:11). At about forty years old, Moses, in a well-thought-out decision motivated by faith, renounced his Egyptian upbringing and associated with his Hebrew brothers and sisters. Granted, the way that Moses tried to save Israel, namely his violent avenging of a mistreated Israelite, was misguided. But after God trained him for another forty years in Midian, Moses was ready to assume his God-given role as leader and deliverer (Exodus 2:11–14; Acts 7:24–29).

Moses risked much by pledging allegiance to God and his people. (The following points come from Daniel Lockwood.) First, Moses gave up an exalted *position*. "Moses ... refused to be called the son of Pharaoh's daughter" (Hebrews 11:24). As the adopted son of the king's daughter, Moses was destined for political greatness, but he relinquished the power and prestige to share in the mistreatment of God's people. Why? Because Moses realized that the accolades of his Egyptian pedigree were fleeting; he longed to be great in the eyes of God, not in the estimation of his peers.

Second, Moses gave up sinful *pleasures*. He chose not "to enjoy the passing pleasures of sin" (v. 25). Make no mistake about it, sin is enjoyable. But the ecstasy of iniquity quickly evaporates. Moses accepted harsh abuse with the Israelites because he believed something better was waiting for him. The Bible says that "the wages of sin is death, but the free gift of God is eternal life in Christ Jesus our Lord" (Romans 6:23). The pleasures of sin last for a moment; the consequences of sin can last a lifetime (or even forever), but divine grace and everlasting life are available to believers. Moses recognized that God provides what sin cannot—true and lasting satisfaction.

Third, Moses gave up priceless *possessions*. He renounced "the treasures of Egypt" (Hebrews 11:26). David McClister describes the wealth of Egypt in the days of Moses: "The brilliant treasures of Egypt during the New Kingdom Period were legendary, as modern archeology has confirmed, and their mention here ... emphasizes the magnitude of Moses's choice and the sacrifice it entailed. What makes Moses's choice so significant is what he had to lose by making it." The Egyptians had "everything." The

Hebrews had "nothing." Moses chose to associate with the latter. Why? Because "he was looking to the reward" (v. 26). The Greek word translated "he was looking" (*apoblepō*) means "to look away from all other objects and to concentrate solely on one thing" (McClister; see LSJ, s.v. "ἀποβλέπω"). Moses disregarded the treasures of Egypt and focused on the divine reward, which in the context of Hebrews 11 probably refers to the unseen, eternal inheritance of heaven (10:32–36; 11:1, 6, 9–10, 13–16).

Moses stood with God and Israel. He suffered "losses," but what he gained far outweighed them. Moses did all these things by faith. This faith allowed him to overcome all obstacles and fears. Oh that we too would sacrifice position, pleasures, and possessions to gain the reward of God and his people!

FAITH THAT CASTS OUT FEAR

Moses, like his parents, was not afraid of Pharaoh: "By faith he left Egypt, not fearing the wrath of the king; for he endured, as seeing him who is unseen" (Hebrews 11:27). Moses bravely left Egypt. But to which flight from Egypt does the author of Hebrews refer—Moses's departure after he killed the Egyptian (Exodus 2:11–15) or his exodus with Israel after the final plague against Egypt (12:29–41)? The first option is seemingly correct, for (1) Hebrews 11 typically follows a chronological order and (2) the wrath of Pharaoh does not appear to be a cause of fear following the final plague against Egypt. However, a potential objection arises with this interpretation: Exodus 2:14 affirms that "Moses was afraid" when he fled from Egypt the first time, whereas Hebrews 11:27 contends that he was not. This is not a contradiction, however, for fear may not have been the cause of his departure or, more likely, Moses may have overcome his fear with faith. (In support of this interpretation, Philo, a Jewish philosopher, and Josephus, a Jewish, defend the courageous faith of Moses; see Philo, *On the Life of Moses* 1.47–50; *Allegorical Interpretation* 3.12–14; Josephus, *Jewish Antiquities* 2.254–257.) Moses did not give up. He refused to tremble before the king of Egypt. Why? Because he could "see" the invisible God. He knew that the Lord was with him. This gave Moses the strength that he needed to face Egyptian hostility, an uncertain future, and delayed deliverance. Moses conquered his fear. Faith in God enables us to do the same. We need only to fix our eyes on God, see him as he is, and draw strength and courage from him.

BEARING THE REPROACH OF CHRIST

Moses ultimately decided to stand with God and his people because he wanted to suffer with Christ. The writer of Hebrews notes that Moses considered "the reproach of Christ" a greater reward than the treasures of Egypt (Hebrews 11:26; see 13:13). The word translated "reproach" (*oneidismos*) means "abuse, insult, or reviling" (BDAG, s.v. "ὀνειδισμός"). So, what is "the reproach of Christ" in Hebrews 11:26? It may be (1) the reproach that Christ himself endured, (2) the reproach that believers suffer on account of Christ, or (3) the reproach that Moses himself endured as a type of the sufferings of Christ. Or it may be a combination of these ideas. By standing with Israel, Moses shared in the tribulation that all Godfearers endure, Jesus Christ himself being the prime example of godly suffering (2 Timothy 3:12; Psalm 69:9; 89:50–51; Colossians 1:24).

Moses, not yet knowing Jesus, chose, to suffer for him, anticipating his reward. The same hope is before us: "If … we suffer with [Christ] … we [will] also be glorified with him" (Romans 8:17; see v. 18; Hebrews 13:13–14). As we bear the reproach of Christ, as Moses did, we anticipate a share in the great reward.

CONCLUSION

Moses pleased God because he (Moses) stood with him and his people. He gave up his exalted position, sinful pleasures, and priceless possessions. God, therefore, blessed him in extraordinary ways; he made Moses the lawgiver and leader of Israel; he showed him the promised land; he allowed him to talk with Jesus on the Mount of Transfiguration; and he will raise Moses (and all the faithful) to eternal glory at the last day. As we follow in the footsteps of Moses by standing with God and his people and bearing the reproach of Christ, we know that we will receive the same divine approval and the same eternal reward.

BIG IDEAS AND APPLICATIONS

- Standing with God and his people is costly. Sacrifice for the cause of Christ!
- Faith triumphs over fear. Be strong and courageous, "seeing" the invisible God through the eyes of faith!
- The reproach of Christ ends in reward. Stand up, stand up for Jesus!

SUGGESTED PRAYER

Promise God that you will choose him and his people over everything else and that you will bear the reproach of Christ. Thank God that your faith gives you courage and hope to do so.

PERSONAL EXAMINATION

Have you ever been afraid to stand with God and his people? If so, why were you anxious to identify yourself as a Christian? If not, during the times that you have aligned yourself with God and his people, even at great loss (real or potential), what encouraged you to do so?

GROUP DISCUSSION

Answer the following questions. Be ready to discuss them as a group.

1. Read Hebrews 3:1–6. Compare Moses and Jesus. In what way(s) was Moses faithful in the house of God?

_____
_____
_____

2. Who were the parents of Moses, and how did they demonstrate their faith in God? Why did they do so? (Hebrews 11:23)

_____
_____
_____

3. What did Moses give up to identify himself with God and his people? Read Luke 14:16–33. What must we be willing to abandon to be a follower of Jesus?

_____
_____
_____

4. How did Moses conquer his fear? Find at least three scriptures that tell us not to be afraid. From these passages, why should we be fearless, and what must we do to become so?

_____
_____
_____

5. What do you think is meant by "the reproach of Christ" in Hebrews 11:26? Why did Moses consider the reproach of Christ greater riches than those of Egypt? Read Hebrews 13:13–14. What are Christians called to bear, and why?

_____
_____
_____

WEEKLY CHALLENGE

Moses resolved to follow God and to help his fellow Israelites. This led to conflict with the idolatrous nation of Egypt. We must align ourselves with Christ and other Christians, even when it results in persecution. This week, if you hear your family and friends blaspheming God and his people, instead of remaining quiet, humbly stand up for them. Be ready to share your experience with the group or with a close friend.

LESSON 10
Faith WAITS ON GOD
MOSES, JOSHUA & ISRAEL

KEY SCRIPTURES
Hebrews 11:28–30; Exodus 12:21–42; 14:10–31;
Joshua 6:1–21;

OPENING SONG
"Teach Me, Lord, to Wait," C. Stuart Hamblen

Do we trust God, even when he asks us to wait? Scripture repeatedly issues the command to wait upon the Lord. The Bible affirms that those who do so will experience God's goodness, joy, salvation, and strength (Lamentations 3:15; Psalm 27:13–14; Isaiah 25:9; 40:31). Hebrews 11 mentions several notable people—Noah, Abraham, Isaac, Joseph, Moses, and the Israelites—who waited for the Lord and received his gracious gifts. In this study, we will consider the perseverance of Moses, Joshua, and Israel. Their examples show us that waiting upon God always yields the best results.

UNTOUCHED BY THE DESTROYER

The Israelites sojourned in Egypt for centuries, and even after the birth of their deliverer Moses, they still had to wait eighty years before God released them from Egyptian oppression. Following a forty-year "exile" in Midian, Moses returned to Egypt and ordered Pharaoh to release God's people. Because Pharaoh refused to acquiesce, God punished him, the Egyptians, and their so-called gods with terrible plagues. The writer of Hebrews focuses on the last of these plagues, the death of the firstborn: "By faith he [Moses] kept the Passover and the sprinkling of the blood, so that he who destroyed the firstborn would not touch them [the Israelites]" (Hebrews 11:28). The night of the first Passover, God judged Egypt and so delivered Israel from slavery (Exodus 11–12). Passover therefore became an annual, memorial feast and "commemorated the turning-point in Israel's existence" (David McClister).

Passover revealed the faith of Moses and Israel. They believed the warning and the promise of God, specifically that judgment was coming on the disobedient Egyptians but that salvation from the destroyer was available to the obedient Israelites who smeared the prescribed blood on the doorposts of their houses. They recognized the necessity of submission, even before God gave them the written law, and obeyed without excuse or doubt. They did not question God's word by raising objections like, "Surely God will not kill the children," or "We didn't have to do anything like this for the other plagues," or "Why in the world would God ask us to put animal blood on our doors?" Moses and Israel understood that God had reasons for doing what he was doing and that their faithfulness to God would stay the hand of the destroyer.

Several months had lapsed from the first plague and the last plague. During that time, Moses and Israel had to wait (and suffer)! Their loyalty to God led them to victory. God protected his people even as he punished the Egyptians. The Israelites would probably have preferred immediate deliverance, but God was showing them (and everyone else) that they were his special people and that he would fight for them. The ultimate proof of this was Passover. The continued observance of this feast reminded Israel of its privileged relationship with God and previewed the salvation that we enjoy in Christ (1 Corinthians 5:7).

FEAR NOT, STAND STILL, AND SEE THE SALVATION OF THE LORD

Following Passover, the exodus began. The Egyptians drove out the Israelites, and God took his people to the shores of the Red Sea (Exodus 13:17–14:9). Meanwhile, however, Pharaoh hardened his heart (again) and pursued Israel. When the Israelites saw the Egyptians, they initially acted in unbelief (14:10–12). "[They] were anything but heroes here. They panic[ked], turning to Moses with harsh complaints" (Daniel Lockwood).

Moses, on the other hand, responded in faith, commanding Israel to wait upon the Lord: "Do not fear! Stand by and see the salvation of the LORD which He will accomplish for you today; for the Egyptians whom you have seen today, you will never see them again forever. The LORD will fight for you while you keep silent" (14:13–14; see vv. 15–18). The angel of God barricaded the camp of Israel so that the Egyptians could not overtake them (vv. 19–20). Moses then stretched his hand over the sea, and God caused a strong wind to blow overnight, parting the water and allowing the Israelites to walk through the sea on dry ground (vv. 21–25). And when their foes tried to follow, God released the waters and drowned the Egyptians (vv. 26–31).

The Israelites were slow to believe. They needed the reassurance of Moses. They had to feel the divinely wrought wind and see the watery corridor. But they learned trust—at least for a time! Their faith was "driven by necessity and confirmed by physical evidence, but it [was] ... faith just the same" (Daniel Lockwood). The writer of Hebrews affirms the saving faith of Israel: "By faith they passed through the Red Sea as though they were passing through dry land; and the Egyptians, when they attempted it, were drowned" (Hebrews 11:29). Israel needed to stand still and be quiet. When they did, God rescued them from disaster.

The Egyptians, on the other hand, persisted in unbelief. They put their confidence in Pharaoh to devastating results. "It was their belief in God and in his word that saved the Israelites, and it was the unbelief and persistent disobedience of the Egyptians that brought on their ruin" (Robert Milligan). Both the Israelites and the Egyptians had to wait for God, but only the former received the reward of salvation because of their faith.

We too must learn to wait upon the Lord—putting aside our fears, standing still, keeping quiet, and watching God work. When we do, he does the "impossible" in, for, and through us. In this sense, the exodus from Egypt and the crossing of the Red Sea foreshadows the Christian experience (1 Corinthians 10:1–4). The same God who saved Israel from Egypt can and will rescue us from sin and peril—if we wait upon him!

A GLARING OMISSION

Following his description of the crossing of the Red Sea, the author of Hebrews skips to the conquest of Jericho (Hebrews 11:29–30). Why omit forty years of Israelite history? He may do so because the journey through the desert is a period of national infidelity. Though God providentially cared for his people as they traveled from Egypt to Sinai and on to the border of Canaan, the Israelites doubted and refused to enter the promised land (Numbers 1:1–14:19). God therefore forced them to wander in the wilderness south of Canaan for forty years, until the faithless generation died (14:20–38).

The New Testament rarely mentions the wilderness wandering, but each time it does, it reminds us that unbelief results in tragedy and heartbreak. Jude warns "that Jesus, who saved a people out of the land of Egypt, afterward destroyed those who did not believe" (Jude 5 ESV). Paul instructs Christians to learn from the failures of the wicked Israelites (1 Corinthians 10:5–11). The writer of Hebrews comes to a similar conclusion: "Therefore, since the promise of entering his rest still stands, let us be careful that none of you be found to have fallen short of it. … Let us, therefore, make every effort to enter that rest, so that no one will perish by following their example of disobedience" (Hebrews 4:1, 11 NIV; see 3:7–19; 4:2–10). These warnings urge us to trust the Lord, wait for his salvation, and look expectantly to the true, promised rest..

THE WALLS CAME TUMBLING DOWN

Hebrews 11 next moves to the destruction of Jericho (Hebrews 11:30). Following the conquest of the land east of the Jordan River, Joshua replaced Moses as the commander of Israel, the people renewed their covenant with God, and God promised to fight their battles for them, if they would put their confidence in him (Joshua 1–5). Jericho was the first city of the campaign.

God gave the Israelites a strange battle plan. He told them to march around the city for seven days (6:1–11). David McClister draws attention to the divine intention behind this unorthodox strategy: "There was no logical connection between the method and results, and God used this method because it required that his people act in faith in his orders." God wanted Israel to trust him. Thankfully, Joshua did not question the Lord, and the army did not object. They obeyed, and the walls collapsed (vv. 12–27). Faith secured victory: "By faith the walls of Jericho fell down after they had been encircled for seven days" (Hebrews 11:30). Israel had to wait upon God, but by trusting him, they conquered Jericho.

We may likewise face seemingly unwinnable battles. The divine path to victory may seem to be illogical and ineffective (e.g., "God wants me to turn the other cheek?!" "Forgive him after what he did?!" "Pray?!"). God knows what he is doing. He never disappoints those who put their faith in him (Isaiah 28:16; Romans 10:11). He breaks down satanic barriers, makes us more than conquerors, and bestows on us an eternal inheritance in the true land of promise. "What then shall we say to these things? If God is for us, who is against us? … But in all these things we overwhelmingly conquer through Him who loved us" (Romans 8:31, 37). We need only to wait upon the Lord.

CONCLUSION

Moses, Joshua, and Israel waited on God. His timing and methods often did not make sense, but they always yielded the best results. We too must learn to trust the Lord, even if it means we must wait. F. B. Meyer offers the following insightful comment: "If God told [us] on the front end how long [we] would wait to find the fulfillment of [our] desire or pleasure or dream, [we would] lose heart. … But He doesn't. He just says, 'Wait. I keep My word. I'm in no hurry. In the process of time, I'm developing you to be ready for the promise.'" Faith waits upon God.

BIG IDEAS AND APPLICATIONS

- God punished the enemies of his people at Passover. Wait for his vengeance!
- God protected his people at the Red Sea. Wait for his rescue!
- God provide his people an inheritance at Jericho. Wait for his victory!

SUGGESTED PRAYER

Praise God for his infinite wisdom and power. Thank him for teaching you to wait. Promise him that you will trust his timing and methods and accept his purpose for your life.

PERSONAL EXAMINATION

Think of a time when you asked God for something but he made you wait. Did you enjoy waiting? Why, or why not? Did you respond in faith or doubt (or both)? What did you learn from the experience?

GROUP DISCUSSION

Answer the following questions. Be ready to discuss them as a group.

1. Describe the first Passover. Why was faith needed to celebrate this Passover? What was the end of those who faithfully observed the first Passover?

2. Read Exodus 14. Who led the Israelites to the (inescapable) shores of the Red Sea? How did the people respond when they saw Pharaoh in pursuit? What did Moses tell Israel to do? What was the result?

_____

_____

_____

3. Why was the generation that came out of Egypt forbidden entrance into the Promised Land? (See Hebrews 3:7–4:11, Jude 5, and 1 Corinthians 10:5–11.) What should we learn from the faithlessness of Israel?

_____

_____

_____

4. How did ancient armies typically conquer walled cities? (You may need to look up the word *siege* in a Bible dictionary or encyclopedia to find the answer to this question.) What was God's battle plan for the conquest of Jericho? What does this Old Testament story teach you about faith?

_____

_____

_____

5. Read Isaiah 40:27–31. How does Isaiah describe God? Whom will the Lord strengthen? What must we do and not do if we want God to help us?

_____

_____

_____

WEEKLY CHALLENGE

Waiting is hard. Read Psalm 27 several times before the next class. What does the psalmist (David) know about God? What does he want from the Lord? What does he encourage others to do? When we face interruptions and delays in life, how can we apply the principles of Psalm 27 to wait (more patiently) upon God? Be ready to share with the group or with a family member or friend what you learn from this psalm and how it is helping you to face an issue in your life.

LESSON 11

Faith GIVES NEW LIFE IN GOD
RAHAB

KEY SCRIPTURES
Hebrews 11:31; Joshua 2:1–24; James 2:14–26;

OPENING SONG
"Trust and Obey," John H. Sammis

God leveled the walls of Jericho because Israel trusted and obeyed him, but the Israelites were not the only victors in the skirmish. By faith, Rahab, a Canaanite prostitute, protected herself and her family from the devastation of the city. What an unexpected addition to the faithful of Hebrews 11! The writer of Hebrews, having previously discussed the belief of the Israelites, concludes his "by faith" discussion with a description of Rahab's faith: "By faith Rahab the harlot did not perish along with those who were disobedient, after she had welcomed the spies in peace" (Hebrews 11:31). God saved Rahab because she professed and practiced faith. Faith not only preserved her life but also prompted her to present her life to God. We must do the same if we wish to live now and in eternity.

A DISOBEDIENT PEOPLE AND AN UNEXPECTED ALLY

By the time that the Israelites entered the Promised Land, the Canaanites had reached the state of moral decay from which there was no hope of redemption. Skeptics who read the story of the conquest often charge God and Israel with bigotry and genocide, but the war against the Canaanites was not an ethnic but a moral cleansing campaign, divine punishment for the immeasurable national wickedness of the Canaanites. Daniel Lockwood describes the religion of Canaan as "infectiously depraved." Archeologists confirm this assessment. Documents from Ugarit, a city in ancient Syria, north of Israel, link Canaanite religion with atrocities such as "religious prostitution" and "child sacrifice" (William LaSor, David Hubbard, and Frederic Bush). God had given the Canaanites centuries to repent of their evil practices, but they were unwilling and only grew worse (Genesis 15:13–16; Leviticus 18:24–25; Deuteronomy 9:4–5). So, when the Israelites surrounded Jericho, the inhabitants did not humble themselves and surrender; they persisted in disobedience and demonic faith, fearing God but fighting against him (Heb 11:31). Only one woman, a common prostitute named Rahab, broke the mold and allied herself with God and his people.

Joshua 2:1–21 and 6:22–25 details most of what we know about Rahab. Rahab first showed faith toward God when Joshua commissioned his two spies to infiltrate and explore Jericho. Rahab, who owned a local brothel, welcomed the spies into her home and protected them from their enemies. When the king of Jericho commanded her to produce the men, she lied about their whereabouts and then sent them away safely. Why would Rahab "betray" her city and stand with God and his people? The simple answer is that she was (or had become) a woman of faith. Her reverence for God compelled her to submit to him and beg for rescue from the coming judgment. The writer of Hebrews describes this commitment to God as faith (Hebrews 11:31). Though everyone else in her city was disobedient and unbelieving, Rahab chose a different course by separating herself from her immoral companions and pledging loyalty to the God of Israel. The conversion of Rahab may surprise some, but it is a powerful illustration of how God effects spiritual transformation in even the so-called worst of sinners who entrust themselves to God and his word.

THE SPIRITUAL TRANSFORMATION OF A PROSTITUTE

The writer of Hebrews probably draws attention to the former occupation of Rahab (1) to distinguish her from any other Rahab in the Old Testament, (2) to highlight the lasting effects of sin, and (3) to celebrate the transformative power of faith. Rahab is not just "Rahab" but "Rahab the harlot" (Hebrews 11:31; see James 2:25). Though some contend that Rahab was merely an innkeeper and not a sex worker, the biblical description is clear. She was a prostitute (*zônâ* in Hebrew and *pornē* in Greek; Joshua 2:1; 6:17, 22, 25; Hebrews 11:31; James 2:25). God obviously abhors harlotry, but "faith," as Daniel King Sr. notes, "has the power to change lives"—even the life of Rahab! Rahab went from being an immoral Canaanite woman—dead in trespasses and sins—to being a Godfearing citizen of Israel—alive in the Lord (Joshua 6:25). But how did this transformation happen?

The spiritual renewal of Rahab occurred because Rahab responded rightly to the revelation of God. Her confession in Joshua 2:9b–11 unites divine communication and human conversion. In other words, Rahab changed because she recognized who God was and what he had determined for her and her people, and she wanted God to rescue her from the ensuing judgment. Rahab knew of the divine intention to give the land to the Israelites; she therefore refused to fight against him or them (v. 9). She had also heard of the power of God—power that parted the Red Sea and crushed the Amorites on the east side of the Jordan; she resolved, then, to honor God and submit to his lordship (vv. 10–11). So then, when Rahab professed and demonstrated her loyalty to God, God listened, justified her, and saved her and her family from destruction. Rahab was still a Canaanite by birth, but God no longer associated her with her unbelieving relatives. She needed to learn the specific demands of the law of Moses, particularly the prohibition against bearing false witness, but God was longsuffering toward her. Finally, though Rahab had to bear the tag of her former lifestyle ("Rahab the harlot"), she abandoned her immorality to join herself to God and his people, even marrying an Israelite. What a transformation faith in God wrought in this woman!

If God reformed Rahab, should we ever think ourselves out of his reach? Absolutely not! God can resurrect the spiritually dead to eternal life in Christ (Ephesians 2:1–10;

see 1 Corinthians 6:9–11). He wants to work in us to mold our wills and motivate our works to be well-pleasing to him (Philippians 2:13; see Titus 2:11–14). But to enjoy the blessing of a new life in Christ, we, like Rahab, must determine to "work out [our] salvation with fear and trembling" (Philippians 2:12). The fear of the Lord moves us from friendship with the world to faithfulness to God and ultimately to freedom from sin and judgment.

JUSTIFIED BY FAITH AND WORKS

Faith saved Rahab, but her faith was not mere mental assent. James reminds us that Rahab's faith included works: "In the same way, was not Rahab the harlot also justified by works when she received the messengers and sent them out by another way?" (James 2:25). While the writer of Hebrews stresses that God saved Rahab because of her faith, James affirms that God justified her because of her works. (Salvation and justification are similar but not identical. Even so, James recognizes substantial overlap between them; cf. James 2:14, 24.) What saved and justified Rahab? Faith or works? Does not Paul say that works cannot save or justify people? Space prevents an in-depth analysis of these questions, but the simple answer is that faith and works are not necessarily in opposition to one another. The writer of Hebrews regularly defines faith as faithfulness to God, which includes corresponding works (Hebrews 10:35–39). James calls attention to the necessity of works because certain ones in his audience were redefining faith in solely intellectual or emotional terms (James 2:14–26). Hebrews and James thus complement Paul. Paul also understands faith to be faithfulness. He never proposes a works-free, that is, an obedience-free, Christianity. When Paul says that works do not save or justify, he is talking about works in which people were making a boast apart from God or Christ (Romans 3:19–31). Hebrews, James, and Paul emphasize differing aspects of faith and works, but their message is the same: Faith and works save and justify. Is it any wonder, then, that Hebrews and James present Rahab as a model of salvation and justification? Rahab believed God, pledged her loyalty to him, and demonstrated her commitment through works. Do we yearn for the salvation and justification that Rahab received? If so, we must do as she did, that is, live by faith and works.

THE PHYSICAL AND SPIRITUAL REWARDS OF FAITH

God rewarded Rahab for her faith. The immediate prize was that she "did not perish along with those who were disobedient," but the divine blessings extended far beyond the initial reward (Hebrews 11:31). God permitted Rahab to join with his people: "Rahab the harlot and her father's household and all she had, Joshua spared; and she has lived in the midst of Israel to this day, for she hid the messengers whom Joshua sent to spy out Jericho" (Joshua 6:25). She not only resided among the Israelites but even married one of them, Salmon. The progeny of Salmon and Rahab played vital roles in the plan of God. Their son was Boaz, their great-great-grandson was David, and their most important descendant was Jesus (Matthew 1:5–6). (Some interpreters argue that the Rahab in Matthew 1:5 is not the Rahab of Hebrews 11:31 and James 2:25

since the Greek spellings of "Rahab" differ in Matthew and Hebrews/James. Spelling inconsistencies are, however, quite common in Scripture, and Matthew presents his Rahab—as he does all the women in the genealogy of Jesus—as a well-known character from the Old Testament. There is no reason to doubt, then, that the Rahab of Matthew 1:5 is Rahab the harlot.) God used Rahab to bring Christ into the world. Few, if any, would have imagined that a Canaanite prostitute would an ancestor of the Messiah, but God demonstrates his grace and "the universality of the gospel" in Rahab (Thomas Hewitt). What a legacy! Lastly, God promises Rahab (and everyone who is faithful to him) an eternal inheritance. No greater prize exists for the people of God. These blessings (salvation, adoption, inheritance) are available today. If we show the same faithfulness to God that Rahab did, we will receive the same rewards.

CONCLUSION

Rahab did not perish with the disobedient because she was a woman of faith (and works). God saved her from sin and judgment, appointed her a place among his people, and granted her with a lasting spiritual legacy. He wants to do the same for us. If we, like Rahab, pledge loyalty to him, he will bring us to life in Christ and craft us into a people of good works. The faithful live because of God. The faithful live for God. Are we faithful to God?

BIG IDEAS AND APPLICATIONS

- God saves sinners who entrust themselves to him and him alone. Fear him!
- God justifies people who demonstrate an active faith. Work for him!
- God rewards the faithful with incomprehensible blessings. Hope in him!

SUGGESTED PRAYER

Thank God that he wants to save you from your sins and the coming judgment. Promise him that you will live a life of faith and works. Thank him for the rewards that he has secured for you.

PERSONAL EXAMINATION

Do you possess a Rahab-like faith, that is, a faith that fears God, works for him, and forsakes disobedience? If so, what has helped you to develop this kind of faith? If not, what can you do today to change and improve?

GROUP DISCUSSION

Answer the following questions. Be ready to discuss them as a group.

1. Read Hebrews 11:31. What was the result of the faith of Rahab? What kind of people died at Jericho? How did Rahab demonstrate that she was loyal to God and Israel?

___

2. List at least two abominations that the Canaanites practices as part of their religion. Why did God wait so long to punish the Canaanites for their wickedness? (See Genesis 15:13–16.) Read Joshua 2:1–21 and 6:22–25. In what way(s) did Rahab resemble the rest of the Canaanites, and in what way(s) did she differ from them?

___

3. Before she joined herself to God and Israel, what was Rahab's occupation? What did Rahab understand that prompted her to commit herself to God? Compare the spiritual transformation of Rahab and that of people today. (See Ephesians 2:1–10, 1 Corinthians 6:9–11, Philippians 2:12–13, and Titus 2:11–14.)

___

4. Read James 2:14–26. What justified Rahab? Explain.

___

5. What physical and spiritual rewards did Rahab receive because of her faith? In what way(s) do we hope for the same rewards?

___

WEEKLY CHALLENGE

Faith changed everything for Rahab. Though Rahab had to take some big risks and make some big changes at first, her commitment to God continued after the destruction of Jericho. She married a husband and raised a child(ren) who loved God. Faith therefore went from the big to the small. If you have already made the big changes, look for small ways to live for God this week. Be ready to share with the class or with a friend how dedicating even these small thoughts and actions to God helped you spiritually.

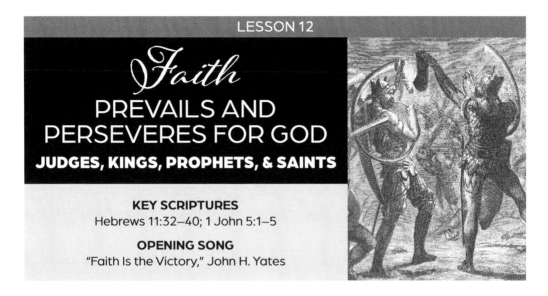

LESSON 12
Faith PREVAILS AND PERSEVERES FOR GOD
JUDGES, KINGS, PROPHETS, & SAINTS

KEY SCRIPTURES
Hebrews 11:32–40; 1 John 5:1–5

OPENING SONG
"Faith Is the Victory," John H. Yates

If the inspired summary of faithful men and women in Heb 11:3–31 felt at all rushed, get ready because the author of Hebrews kicks it into high gear in verses 32–40! Hebrews 11:32–40 quickly catalogs famous judges, kings, and prophets, along with a host of other unnamed saints. The author begins with this rhetorical question: "And what more shall I say?" In other words, "How much more do I need to say?" (NLT). He knows that he made the point but adds a few more people to the list to round off his discussion. Why add them? Because these men and women prevailed and persevered through their faith in God.

REPRESENTATIVES OF VICTORIOUS FAITH

Hebrews 11:32–40 is a representative, not a comprehensive, list of the faithful, though the presence of some of the people in this list may shock us. The phrase "time will fail me" (v. 32) is "a common rhetorical clue to an audience that the speaker [is] going to condense the following material" (David McClister). Consequently, the author of Hebrews includes only a select number of judges, kings, prophets, and saints. He begins with six men: Gideon, Barak, Samson, Jephthah, David, Samuel (v. 32). It comes as no surprise that men such as Samuel and David are on the list, but what of Barak, Gideon, Jephthah, and Samson?! How did these men with their recorded failures find their way into Hebrews 11? We will answer these questions later. Clearly, however, the writer of Hebrews wants to demonstrate that faith ensures victory for the people of God—regardless of whether the faith of certain individuals is expected or unexpected and whether their victories were immediate and physical or delayed and eternal. What, then, should we learn about faith from the men and women of Hebrews 11:32–40?

SOME PREVAILED

First, we learn that faith sometimes empowers believers to overcome insurmountable odds to conquer foes and escape death (Hebrews 11:33–35a). Gideon destroyed the altar of Baal and faced the Midianites with only three hundred men (Judges 6:25–32; 7:2–8:21). Barak defeated the Canaanites and joined the victory song of Deborah (4:11–5:31). Samson slaughtered the Philistines and relied on God—albeit imperfectly—through prayer (15:14–20; 16:28–31). Jephthah routed the Ammonites (11:1–33). David slew "his tens of thousands" of Philistines, Amalekites, Moabites, Arameans, and Edomites and escaped the sword of Saul (2 Samuel 18:7; cf. 8:1–14). Samuel not only served as a prophet of God but also vanquished the Philistines with the sword of Israel and his own prayers and sacrifices (1 Samuel 7:3–14). The list could go on. "By faith [they] conquered kingdoms, performed acts of righteousness, obtained promises, shut the mouths of lions, quenched the power of fire, escaped the edge of the sword, from weakness were made strong, became mighty in war, put foreign armies to flight. Women received back their dead by resurrection" (Hebrews 11:33–35a). These men and women won great physical and spiritual victories.

But what should we make of the obvious weaknesses and failures of certain men and women in Hebrews 11:32–35a? Gideon initially cowered in fear, needed miraculous signs, and "sent a false signal to both the people and his son when he acted like a typical Canaanite king" (Robert Chisholm, Jr.; Judges 6:11–40; 7:9–14; 8:22–35). Barak refused to fight until Deborah accompanied him (4:6–10). Even mentioning the name "Samson" reminds us of his repeated moral catastrophes (14:1–16:31). Jephthah sacrificed his daughter (11:29–40). David committed adultery and murder (2 Samuel 11:1–27). Samuel appointed his wayward sons as judges (1 Sam 8:1–3). Again, the list could go on. So, why does the writer of Hebrews include weak and sinful people as examples of faith? Because he wants his wavering (and perhaps even wayward) audience to overcome their own weaknesses and sins and prove faithful to God. Faith empowered people to triumph over both the world and themselves—their anger, hatred, lust, cowardice, or whatever vice that they indulge. As we pledge our loyalty to God, we will enjoy an even greater victory that did the people of old (1 John 5:1–5).

How can we prevail over evil forces and secure spiritual victory? Like the men and women of Hebrews 11:32–35a, we must establish our confidence in God, prioritize prayer to him, and act when the time is right. Looking to the example of our spiritual predecessors, we grow in our confidence that we can win the battles, our personal and collective victories encourage us to keep fighting, and God himself assures us that we will reign with Christ. Prevail!

OTHERS PERSEVERED

Next, we learn that faith sometimes requires believers to face terrible hardship, even death, for the cause of Christ but that it also enables them to persevere through these difficulties (Hebrews 11:35b–38). So, though the men and women of Hebrews 11:32–35a triumphed over their foes, those of verses 35b–38 did not experience immediate deliverance. The author of Hebrews underscores the contrast between those who "won" and those who "lost" with the simple phrase "but others…" (v. 35b NET; cf. BDAG, s.v. "δέ"). What a heart-breaking conjunction! God allowed his faithful people to suffer. Why? How could a loving God force/allow his people to meet adversity?

People have wrestled with the problem of suffering for nearly as long as people have existed, but the fact that the faithful (and the unfaithful) suffer does not necessarily deny the existence of God or call his goodness into question. Believers know that God will eventually right all wrongs and reward those who have diligently sought him (v. 6). Faith supports this unseen hope (v. 1). God approves of loyal sufferers and promises them something better in eternity (v. 39a; cf. vv. 35b, 40). The author of Hebrews thus intends

to impress, not depress, his readers. These final representatives of faith in Hebrews 11 ought to encourage us to persevere regardless of what we are suffering. The exhortation echoes to the present, "If they persisted in faithfulness to God, you can too. Don't give up!"

Who are the faithful in 11:35b–38, and how did they show their allegiance to God? While we meet some of them in the biblical record itself, many are only known through secular history, particularly in the Apocrypha and the Pseudepigrapha. The fact that Hebrews 11 alludes to nonbiblical literature does mean that the author believes that God inspired these books. It does prove, however, that even in the so-called Years of Silence, men and women continued to demonstrate loyalty to God. Hebrews 11:35b–38 summarizes the atrocities that these saints faced:

> But others were tortured, not accepting release, to obtain resurrection to a better life. And others experienced mocking and flogging, and even chains and imprisonment. They were stoned, sawed apart, murdered with the sword; they went about in sheepskins and goatskins; they were destitute, afflicted, ill-treated (the world was not worthy of them); they wandered in deserts and mountains and caves and openings in the earth. (NET)

These descriptions apply to a host of named (e.g., Elijah, Elisha, Isaiah, Jeremiah, Uriah) and unnamed saints, but "time will fail me" to recount the various biblical and nonbiblical characters who endured such hostilities. Permit me, then, to mention two resolute Jews who refused to compromise their convictions during the time between the Testaments: Eleazar and an unnamed mother of seven martyrs (2 Maccabees 6:18–31; 7:1–41).

First, the pagan Greeks tried to force Eleazar to eat pork. Eleazar, knowing that torture and death awaited him, refused and with his dying breath said, "It is clear to the Lord in his holy knowledge that, though I might have been saved from death, I am enduring terrible sufferings in my body under this beating, but in my soul I am glad to suffer these things because I fear him" (2 Maccabees 6:30 NRSV). Second, the mother of the seven martyrs watched as her sons died one by one but still encouraged them not to waver in their commitment to God. "The mother was especially admirable and worthy of honorable memory. Although she saw her seven sons perish within a single day, she bore it with good courage because of her hope in the Lord" (2 Maccabees 7:20 NRSV). Eleazar and the mother did not prevail here and now, but they persevered. Why? Because they feared God and hoped in "an everlasting renewal of life" (v. 9 NRSV; cf. v. 14), that is, "a better resurrection" (Hebrews 11:35b).

The original readers of Hebrews were facing terrible oppression. They needed to remind themselves that faithfulness to God is sometimes painful, that God purposely allows his people to suffer, that endurance is necessary, but that the final victory is sure. We need these same reminders today in a world that is becoming increasingly antagonistic toward Christianity. May we resolve now to persevere as our "fathers" and "mothers" in the faith did before us!

APPROVED BUT NOT PERFECTED

Hebrews 11:39–40 concludes, "And all these, having gained approval through their faith, did not receive what was promised, because God had provided something better for us, so that apart from us they would not be made perfect." These faithful men and women prevailed and persevered, but they had not yet attained perfection. Perfection comes only in Christ. They and we attain the promised perfection together, though we yet anticipate ultimate perfection. Joining the ranks of the faithful, we trust that one day we will traverse the final threshold together and receive our victory crown and eternal inheritance.

CONCLUSION

The final representatives of faith in Hebrews 11 reveal the power of faith. Some prevailed, others did not, but they and we together see perfection in Christ if we persevere to the end. Whatever we face in this life, whether good or evil, the legacy of faithful judges, kings, prophets, and saints confirms the hope of Hebrews 10:39: "We are not of those who shrink back to destruction, but of those who have faith to the preserving of the soul." Indeed, "faith is the victory!" Do we possess faith that prevails and perseveres? We can. We must. Let us prepare now so that when the time comes when we must persevere, we will prevail through faith!

BIG IDEAS AND APPLICATIONS

- God sometimes permits the faithful to prevail. Fight by faith!
- God sometimes allows the faithful to "fail." Suffer by faith!
- God always receives and perfects the faithful. Endure to the end!

SUGGESTED PRAYER

Promise God that you will persevere no matter the circumstance. Thank God that he provides the victory in Christ through faith. Profess your steadfast love to him.

PERSONAL EXAMINATION

Do you feel sure or unsure that you have become victorious in Christ? Why? Are you prepared to suffer because of your faith? Why, or why not? What can you do to strengthen your resolve?

_____
_____
_____
_____

GROUP DISCUSSION

Answer the following questions. Be ready to discuss them as a group.

1. Read Hebrews 11:32–38. Besides the men mentioned by name, who comes to mind when you read these descriptions? Which person(s) inspires you the most, and why?

_____
_____
_____

2. What are some of the victories that the men and women of Hebrews 11:32–35b won? How did they show their faith in God before or during these victories? (You may need to review the Old Testament passages concerning these people to answer the preceding question.) Compare their enemies, battles, and triumphs with those that we experience today. What can we learn from the similarities and differences?

_____
_____
_____

3. List some of the weaknesses and sins committed by the people in Hebrews 11:32–35b. Why do you think the author of Hebrews designated these men and women as examples of faith if they sometimes failed spiritually?

_____
_____
_____

4. Why does God allow his faithful ones to suffer? What kinds of hostilities did the people of Hebrews 11:35b–38 face? What kinds of hostilities might we face in the future, and what does the faithfulness of the ancients encourage us to do?

_____
_____
_____

5. Read Hebrews 11:39–40. What do the people of God gain through faith? What do the people of God receive in Christ? How does the hope of present and future perfection motivate you to fight your spiritual battles and to endure the resulting persecution?

_____
_____
_____

WEEKLY CHALLENGE

Faith fights for what is right and endures hostility nobly. Few, if any, of us have faced the level of oppression that our "fathers" and "mothers" of Hebrews 11:32–38 endured and overcame, but someday we may have our own set of enemies demanding that we compromise our convictions. It may come as social, economic, or physical persecution when we refuse to promote abortion-on-demand, misguided notions of social justice, feminist ideology, or homosexuality and transgenderism. We simply do not know what is coming, but we must know now where we stand—and that place must be with God! Brainstorm ways that you can prepare now to persevere when the problems arise. Be ready to share your ideas with the group or with a friend or family member, and then add their ideas to your own to create a plan of action.

LESSON 13

Faith FOCUSES ON GOD
JESUS

KEY SCRIPTURES
Hebrews 12:1–3; 1 Corinthians 9:24–27;
Philippians 2:5–13

OPENING SONG
"My Faith Looks Up to Thee," Ray Palmer

The chapter division between Hebrews 11:40 and 12:1 is somewhat unfortunate. The author of Hebrews teases the race metaphor in 11:39–40 and then fully develops it in 12:1–3. He has not, however, abandoned his focus on faith. He writes,

> Therefore, since we have so great a cloud of witnesses surrounding us, let us also lay aside every encumbrance and the sin which so easily entangles us, and let us run with endurance the race that is set before us, fixing our eyes on Jesus, the author and perfecter of faith, who for the joy set before Him endured the cross, despising the shame, and has sat down at the right hand of the throne of God. For consider Him who has endured such hostility by sinners against Himself, so that you will not grow weary and lose heart. (12:1–3)

The writer of Hebrews knows the threatening circumstances that his readers are facing. He wants to encourage them and enliven their faith. He therefore points them not only to the cloud of witnesses in Hebrews 11 but also—and more importantly—to the premier example of faith, Jesus Christ, and in this way teaches one final lesson about faith: faith focuses on God (and Jesus). Only by fixing our eyes on the Lord can we stay strong and reach the goal.

THE RACE SET BEFORE US

The author of Hebrews depicts the struggle that his readers are facing as a race. Athletic metaphors are common in Scripture. For instance, Paul mentions the Isthmian (or perhaps the Olympic) games, specifically the footraces, to illustrate the value of self-control (1 Corinthians 9:24–27). Moreover, just before his death, he pictures his life in terms of a course (and a sacrifice and a battle) that he is soon to complete (2 Timothy 4:6–8; cf. Acts 20:24). Interestingly, of the key texts that describe the life of disciples in terms of a race, only 2 Timothy 4:7 uses the Greek word for "race" (*dromos*). Clearly, 1 Corinthians 9:24, 26 and Hebrews 12:1 are using the race metaphor too since they both use the verb for "run" (*trechō*), but the nouns translated "race" in these passages are literally "stadium" (*stadion*, 1 Corinthians 9:24 NET) and "fight" (*agōn*, Hebrews

12:1 DRB). The use of "fight" (or "struggle") in Hebrews 12:1 is striking. The writer of Hebrews proceeds to describe their "fight" as "struggle against sin" (v. 4).

The faithful men and women of Hebrews 11, the "great cloud of witnesses" (12:1 NET), have blazed a trail for subsequent generations of Christians and now fill the arena. Consequently, we are not alone in our struggle. Daniel King, Sr. eloquently notes that "nothing is so disheartening as a lonely struggle. ... This unseen cloud of witnesses is intended as a source of inspiration for the disheartened and discouraged readers." Our forebearers are "like ex-players who are now coaching us as we go through the same struggles in which they once participated, telling us about the difficulties ahead of us and thus preparing and encouraging us to endure them" (David McClister). Of course, Jesus is the premier example, "the author and perfecter of faith," and we ultimately follow his lead (v. 2), but we will discuss his place in the metaphor below. The witnesses (and Christ) have run the race. God expects us to pick up the baton and run the next leg of the course.

As an aside, Hebrews 12:1 describes the race as having been "set before us." Who places this struggle before us? In a sense, sinners do (v. 3). Ultimately, however, God does. Granted, God himself does not tempt people to sin (James 1:13). He does not seek downfall of his people. Rather, he supplies "every good gift and every perfect gift" (v. 17 NKJV). Still, he treats his followers as sons, meaning that he sometimes permits us to face hardships to grow our capacity to persevere (James 1:2–4; Hebrews 12:5–11). What does God say to us as we become weary contestants in the race? He, first, tells us to remove additional burdens, "every encumbrance and the sin which so easily entangles us" and to run with endurance by "fixing our eyes on Jesus" (Hebrews 12:1–2).

THE AUTHOR AND PERFECTER OF FAITH

Jesus is the focus of Hebrews. No wonder we must fix our eyes on him! The author of Hebrews highlights Christ's deity, humanity, sonship, and priesthood—and the list goes on. Hebrews 12:2 uniquely describes Jesus as "the author and perfecter of faith," a fitting conclusion to Hebrews 11 and strong consolation for weary disciples of Christ.

Jesus is the author of faith. The word translated "author" (*archēgos*) occurs four times in the New Testament (Acts 3:15; 5:31; Hebrews 2:10; 12:2). An "author" originates or leads (or simply exemplifies). Hebrews 12:2 envisions a Jesus who precedes the faithful in Hebrews 11 and pioneers loyalty to the Father. Jesus is also the perfecter of faith. The word translated "perfecter" (*teleiōtēs*) occurs only here in the New Testament (12:2). A "perfecter" is a "finisher" (NKJV). Jesus "brings faith to its highest attainment, either in himself as an example or in others through his high priestly ministry" (Friberg, s.v. "τελειωτής"). He exemplifies faith from start to finish. The men and women of old demonstrated certain aspects of faith; Jesus embodies every aspect of faith. He "stands as the capstone of the list of [Hebrews 11]. ... [T]he people mentioned in [chapter] 11 only 'saw' (by faith) the finish line and the reward for completion in the future, ahead of them, [but] Jesus has actually crossed the finish line and has reached the heavenly goal itself" (David McClister). This is why God tells us to look to Christ.

"Fixing our eyes on Jesus" is the only path to victory. The witnesses to faith are inspiring, the encumbrances of sin are distracting, but Jesus enables us to finish the race that the men and women of old only started and to remove every spiritual obstacle. So, how do we fix our eyes on Christ? Well, what did the incarnate Jesus do to set his gaze on the Father? He prayed to the Father (5:7a). He honored (or worshiped) him (v. 7b). He learned from him (v. 8). We focus on Christ (and God) in the same ways. We do what the author and perfecter of faith did… including bearing a shameful cross.

A CROSS FOR A CROWN

The path to the crown always passes under the shadow of the cross. It did for Jesus. It does for us. This is why we must fix our eyes on him. How was he able to endure the cross? What did he do? His "success in faithfully enduring the hardships of life … is attributed to his determination to reach the reward God had promised him. This is described in two complementary ways. First, he looked to the joy that was before him, a delight that consisted of heavenly glory with the Father (see John 17:5). Second, he disregarded the shame of the cross" (David McClister). Though grammatically "the joy set before Him" could be what Jesus was experiencing in the presence of God before his time on earth, the focus seems to be on what he knew lay beyond the cross. Just as the race and its reward are "set before us," so also the cross and subsequent joy were "set before him" (Hebrews 12:1, 2). He endured. So must we. Only then can we receive what he received, joy and exaltation.

The mention of faith, joy, endurance, and shame in Hebrews 12:2 is not haphazard or coincidental. The author of Hebrews purposefully weaves these themes together to exhort his readers. Jesus was faithful to the Father. Jesus knew that joy awaited him and therefore endured a shameful death to take hold of it. Jesus won his contest and now reigns with God (v. 2; see 1:3–4; Philippians 2:5–11). What of us? Jesus promises us a crown, but we must first bear the burden and reproach of his cross before we can receive it (Hebrews 2:9–10; see Philippians 2:12–13). Will we falter at the finish line? Will the jeers of the wicked shame us into apostasy? Or will we fix our eyes on Jesus, glory in his (and our) cross, despise the shame of the faithless, and receive from Christ the victory crown? (See also 1 Corinthians 9:24–27, 2 Timothy 4:6–8, and Revelation 2:9–11.)

ENCOURAGEMENT NEEDED TO WIN THE CONTEST

The author of Hebrews closes his discussion of faith with the following imperative: "consider" (Hebrews 12:3). The word translated "consider" (*analogizomai*) occurs only here in the New Testament. In the Septuagint, the Greek translation of the Hebrew Bible, it occurs once and describes the carelessness of idolators (Isaiah 44:19). "Consider" is a thinking word. It conveys the idea of attentiveness. (See Danker, s.v. "ἀναλογίζομαι."). To refuse to consider Christ is to weigh anchor without a destination and to ensure drifting to destruction (Hebrews 2:1; see 12:25). Returning to the race metaphor, to focus on Jesus is to see how he ran his course and make him the goal of our struggle.

The contest is fierce. The adversary is vicious. We must consider Christ who suffered yet persevered "so that [we] will not grow weary and lose heart" (Hebrews 12:3; see v. 5; Galatians 6:9). Jesus wore himself out in service to God and his people, but he did not succumb to fatigue. He persevered. He finished the race. We must learn from Christ how to persist lest we give up. We must push through the pain (hostility), fight to the finish, and fling ourselves at the feet of Jesus. Then and only then will he pick us up and place the victory crown on our head. We can finish the race of faith… by faith. Jesus has shown us how. He is the encouragement that we need to win.

CONCLUSION

Many men and women have finished their segment of the race of faith, but a portion still lies before us. How will we fare? Will we wear out and give up, or will we fight to the finish line and receive the prize? Looking to the saints of old is helpful, but they pale in comparison to the author and perfecter of faith, Jesus Christ. The author of Hebrews urges us to fix our eyes on Jesus. By focusing on him, we ensure our victory. Jesus himself says, "Be faithful unto death, and I will give you the crown of life" (Revelation 2:10 ESV). Amen. Let it be so for each of us.

BIG IDEAS AND APPLICATIONS

- The faithful men and women of old have completed their part of the race. Learn from them and run with endurance!
- Jesus is the premier example of faithfulness. Fix your eyes on him and follow his lead!
- God rewarded Christ with a victory crown after he (Jesus) endured the cross and its shame. He will do the same for us. Be faithful to the very end!

SUGGESTED PRAYER

Promise God that you will learn from your "fathers" and "mothers" in the faith, particularly from Jesus—the author and perfecter of faith. Praise God and Christ for their faithfulness. Promise God that you will focus on Jesus and persevere so that you can reach the goal.

PERSONAL EXAMINATION

What burdens or sins, if any, are weighing you down as you run the race of faith? How will you rid yourself of these hindrances? What can you do today to fix your eyes upon Jesus?

_____
_____
_____
_____

GROUP DISCUSSION

Answer the following questions. Be ready to discuss them as a group.

1. Read 1 Corinthians 9:24–27, 2 Timothy 4:6–8, and Hebrews 12:1–3. Why is the race metaphor a fitting illustration of Christianity? To whom does "the great cloud of witnesses" refer, are they people who make up this group merely spectators, and how does they encourage us to run the race?

_____
_____
_____

2. What does it mean that Jesus is "the author and perfecter of faith," and what should this description of Christ motivate us to do? What are some ways by which we may fix our eyes on Jesus? (See Hebrews 5:7–9.)

_____
_____
_____

3. Read Luke 9:23–26. Though a cross and crucifixion represents a shameful death, what does Jesus expect his followers to do? Why, and how do we do so? (See also Luke 14:26–27 and Galatians 2:20, 5:24, and 6:14.) What will faithful followers of Christ receive when they finish the race? (See 1 Corinthians 9:25, 2 Timothy 4:8, James 1:12, 1 Peter 5:4, and Revelation 2:10 and 3:11.)

_____
_____
_____

4. Read Hebrews 12:3. What does it mean to "consider" Jesus? How do we do so? What will we avoid if we consider Jesus?

_____
_____
_____

5. How has a study of Hebrews 11 strengthened your faith?

WEEKLY CHALLENGE

Jesus focused on his Father. He always did what was pleasing to him, even submitting to the shameful death of the cross. The author of Hebrews calls us to fix our eyes on Jesus, accept the reproach of Christ, and receive the reward. Memorize 2 Timothy 4:7–8. Recite it every day for the next week. Think about it as you prepare yourself to face hardship. Then read and discuss it with a family member or friend. Encourage him or her to commit him- or herself to Christ.

CONCLUSION

The men and women of Hebrews 11 are (or can become) our "fathers" and "mothers" in the faith. When we pledge loyalty to Jesus Christ, as they did to God, we join a new spiritual family. Of course, God is the Father of fathers, but our new "parents" (and "siblings") teach us how to be his children. Anyone can be a part of this family:

> Hebrews 11 implicitly functions as a genealogy which legitimates the Christian audience by providing them with a biblical ancestry. … The heroes derive their status from πίστις ["faith"], not from any national role or office. Πίστις ["Faith"] allows the author to establish a non-national, salvation-historical trajectory which includes the Hebrews community. (Michelle Eisenbaum)

Have you joined the family of faith? An eternal inheritance awaits those who embrace the same kind of faith as Abraham, Moses, David, and Jesus—and all the other "heroes" of Hebrews 11. Our "fathers" and "mothers" still speak, if only we will listen.

We close our study of Hebrews 11 with the following hymn by John Needham (1768): "Rise, O My Soul, Pursue the Path." The lyrics of this song, though set to various melodies (e.g., ARLINGTON = "Am I a Soldier of the Cross?"), sum up and apply the themes that we have explored:

> Rise, O my soul, pursue the path
> By ancient heroes trod;
> Ambitious view those holy men
> Who lived and walked with God.
>
> Though dead, they speak in reason's ear,
> And in example live;
> Their faith, and hope, and mighty deeds
> Still fresh instruction give.
> Say, by whose strength their feeble flesh,
> Such various toils sustained;
> Say, by what means these heirs of grace,
> Immortal triumphs gained.
>
> 'Twas through the Lamb's most precious blood
> They conquered ev'ry foe;
> And to His power and matchless grace
> Their crowns and honors owe.
>
> Warmed by the love that stirred their breasts
> We shall be heroes, too;
> Inspired by equal faith and zeal,
> What wonders we shall do.

The world and flesh shall be denied,
Nor shall we dread the cross;
Pleased that our future gains increase,
By ev'ry present loss.

Lord, may I ever keep in view
The patterns Thou hast giv'n,
And ne'er forsake the blessed road
That led them safe to heav'n.

Will we pursue the path? Will we follow in the footsteps of our faithful "fathers" and "mothers"? Will we be "heroes" who do mighty works for God? We can… by faith. And when we do, the "faith of our fathers" will be "living still" and "we will be true to [it] till death."

WORKS CONSULTED

Brown, Francis, S. R. Driver, Charles A. Briggs et al. *A Hebrew and English Lexicon of the Old Testament*. Boston: Houghton Mifflin, 1907.

Bruce, F. F. *The Epistle to the Hebrews*. NICNT. Grand Rapids: Eerdmans, 1964.

Carson, D. A., and Douglas J. Moo. *An Introduction to the New Testament*. 2nd ed. Grand Rapids: Zondervan, 2005.

Chisholm, Robert B. *From Exegesis to Exposition: A Practical Guide to Using Biblical Hebrew*. Grand Rapids: Baker Books, 1998.

Churchill, Winston. "Never Give In, Never, Never, Never." National Churchill Museum. https://www.nationalchurchillmuseum.org/never-give-in-never-never-never.html.

Cockerill, Gareth Lee. *The Epistle to the Hebrews*. NICNT. Grand Rapids: Eerdmans, 2012.

Cosby, Michael R. "The Rhetorical Composition of Hebrews 11." JBL 107 (1988): 257–73.

Danker, Frederick W., Walter Bauer, William F. Arndt, and F. Wilbur Gingrich. *Greek-English Lexicon of the New Testament and Other Early Christian Literature*. 3rd ed. Chicago: University of Chicago Press, 2000.

Danker, Frederick W., and Kathryn Krug. *The Concise Greek-English Lexicon of the New Testament*. Chicago: University of Chicago Press, 2009.

Delitzsch, Franz. *Commentary on the Epistle to the Hebrews*. Translated by Thomas L. Kingsbury. 2 vols. Edinburgh: T&T Clark, 1874–1876.

Eisenbaum, Michelle. *The Jewish Heroes of Christian History: Hebrews 11 in Literary Context*. SBLDS 156. Atlanta: Scholars Press, 1997.

Ellingworth, Paul. *The Epistle to the Hebrews: A Commentary on the Greek Text*. NIGTC. Grand Rapids: Eerdmans; Carlisle: Paternoster, 1993.

Friberg, Timothy, Barbara Friberg, and Neva F. Miller. *Analytical Lexicon of the Greek New Testament*. 18th ed. Grand Rapids: Baker Books, 2000.

Harris, Dana M. *Hebrews*. EGGNT. Nashville: B&H Academic, 2019.

Hewitt, Thomas. *Epistle to the Hebrews* (Grand Rapids: Eerdmans, 1970).

Holladay, William L. *A Concise Hebrew and Aramaic Lexicon of the Old Testament*. Grand Rapids: Eerdmans; Leiden: Brill, 1988.

"How old was Isaac when Abraham almost sacrificed him?" Got Questions Ministries, https://www.gotquestions.org/how-old-was-Isaac.html.

Johnson, Luke Timothy. *Hebrews: A Commentary*. Louisville: Westminster John Knox, 2006.

Johnson, William G. "The Pilgrimage Motif in the Book of Hebrews." JBL 97 (1978): 239–51.

Lane, William L. *Hebrews: A Call to Commitment*. Vancouver: Regent College Publishing, 1985.

King, Daniel H., Sr. *The Book of Hebrews*. Truth Commentaries. Bowling Green, KY: Guardian of Truth Foundation, 2008.

Kittel, Gerhard, and Gerhard Friedrich, eds. *Theological Dictionary of the New Testament*. Translated by Geoffrey W. Bromiley. 10 vols. Grand Rapids: Eerdmans, 1964–1976.

LaSor, William Sanford, David Allan Hubbard, and Frederic William Bush. *Old Testament Survey: The Message, Form, and Background of the Old Testament*. 2nd ed. Grand Rapids: Eerdmans, 1996.

Liddell, Henry George, Robert Scott, and Henry Stuart Jones. *A Greek-English Lexicon*. 9th ed. Oxford: Clarendon, 1940.

Lockwood, Daniel R. *Unlikely Heroes: Ordinary People with Extraordinary Faith, A Biblical and Personal Reflection on Hebrews* 11. Portland, OR: Multnomah University, 2012.

Lünemann, Gottlieb. *Critical and Exegetical Handbook to the Epistle to the Hebrews*. Translated by Maurice J. Evans. Edinburgh: T&T Clark, 1882.

Machen, J. Gresham. *New Testament Greek for Beginners*. 2nd edition. Edited by Dan G. McCartney. Upper Saddle River, NJ: Pearson/Prentice Hall, 2004.

McClister, David. *A Commentary on Hebrews*. Temple Terrace, FL: Florida College Press, 2010.

Milligan, Robert. *A Commentary on the Epistle to the Hebrews*. Gospel Advocate. Nashville: Gospel Advocate, 1977.

Metzger, Bruce M. *A Textual Commentary on the Greek New Testament*. 2nd ed. Stuttgart: Deutsche Bibelgesellschaft, 1994.

Moltmann, Jürgen. *A Theology of Hope: On the Ground and the Implications of a Christian Eschatology*. Translated by James W. Leitch. Minneapolis: Fortress, 1993.

Mounce, William D. *Mounce's Complete Expository Dictionary of Old and New Testament Words*. Grand Rapids: Zondervan, 2006.

Orr, James et al., eds. *The International Standard Bible Encyclopedia*. 2nd ed. Edited by Melvin Grove Kyle. 5 vols. Grand Rapids: Eerdmans, 1939.

Rowell, Edward K., ed. *1001 Quotes, Illustrations, and Humorous Stories for Preachers, Teachers, and Writers*. Grand Rapids: Baker Books, 2007.

Smyth, H. W. *Greek Grammar*. Rev. ed. Edited by Gordon M. Messing. Cambridge, MA: Harvard University Press, 1956.

Swindoll, Charles, R. *Swindoll's Ultimate Book of Illustrations & Quotes*. Nashville: Nelson, 1998.

Thayer, John Henry, ed. *A Greek-English Lexicon of the New Testament*. Rev. and enl. ed. New York: American Book, 1886.

Thielman, Frank. *Theology of the New Testament*. Grand Rapids: Zondervan, 2005.

Thiessen, Matthew. "Hebrews and the End of the Exodus." NovT 49 (2007): 353–69.

Thompson, James W. *Hebrews*. Paideia. Grand Rapids: Baker Academic, 2008.

Vincent, Marvin R. *Vincent's Word Studies in the New Testament*. New York: Charles Schribner's Sons, 1887.

Wallace, Daniel B. *Greek Grammar Beyond the Basics*. Grand Rapids: Zondervan, 1996.

Walke, Bruce, and Charles Yu. *An Old Testament Theology*. Grand Rapids: Zondervan, 2007.

Young, David. *A Little Guide to a Big Life*. Round Rock, TX: Wind Runner, 2015.

Made in the USA
Columbia, SC
13 June 2025

59210819R00050